WORLD BANK STAFF WORKING PAPERS
Number 597

Poverty, Undernutrition, and Hunger

The World Bank
Washington, D.C., U.S.A.

This is a working document published informally by the World Bank. To present the results of research with the least possible delay, the typescript has not been prepared in accordance with the procedures appropriate to formal printed texts, and the World Bank accepts no responsibility for errors. The publication is supplied at a token charge to defray part of the cost of manufacture and distribution.

The views and interpretations in this document are those of the author(s) and should not be attributed to the World Bank, to its affiliated organizations, or to any individual acting on their behalf. Any maps used have been prepared solely for the convenience of the readers; the denominations used and the boundaries shown do not imply, on the part of the World Bank and its affiliates, any judgment on the legal status of any territory or any endorsement or acceptance of such boundaries.

The full range of World Bank publications is described in the *Catalog of World Bank Publications*; the continuing research program of the Bank is outlined in *World Bank Research Program: Abstracts of Current Studies*. Both booklets are updated annually; the most recent edition of each is available without charge from the Publications Distribution Unit of the Bank in Washington or from the European Office of the Bank, 66, avenue d'Iéna, 75116 Paris, France.

Michael Lipton is professorial fellow in economics in the Institute of Development Studies, University of Sussex, and a consultant to the World Bank.

Library of Congress Cataloging in Publication Data

Lipton, Michael.
    Poverty, undernutrition, and hunger.

    (World Bank staff working papers ; 597)
    Bibliography: p.
    1. Underdeveloped areas--Poor--Nutrition. I. Title.
II. Series.
TX360.5.L56 1983   363.8'2'091724   83-10622
ISBN 0-8213-0204-3

ABSTRACT

This is one of four Working Papers on characteristics of poor and ultra-poor people (see General Introduction). It identifies (a) food-related indicators of how many people are ultra-poor and moderately poor, and (b) these people's nutritional characteristics. To see if income is getting to "the poor", we need a scalar measure of absolute household poverty. Given normal spending patterns, "capacity to afford enough calories to maintain health and performance" best indicates absence of ultra-poverty. It normally prevails whenever household outlay - with about 80% spent on food - meets below 80% of 1973 FAO/WHO caloric requirements. If such outlay patterns meet 80-100% of requirements, the household is probably sometimes hungry, and certainly often unable to afford non-food needs, but seldom "ultra-poor" - at income-induced nutritional risk to health or performance. We call it "moderately poor".

80% of 1973 requirements normally suffices to avoid undernutrition (though not hunger), for five reasons. First, post-1973 evidence suggests lower requirements for "reference" Western persons. Second, more reduction is needed for climates, body-weights and age-structures in poor households in developing countries. Third, persons who ingest below-average calories may do so because requirements too are below average. Fourth, reduced intakes on a person-day may, within limits, increase food-to-work conversion efficiency. Finally, most evidence suggests that (though "moderate" states can be painful and unpleasant) only anthropometrically "severe" undernutrition associated with very low intakes and ultra-poverty - independently endangers health and performance.

The distinction between ultra-poverty (and resulting risk of under-nutrition) and poverty (and risk of hunger) permits them to be "measured" in any of three ways - by nutritional correlates, by income or outlay levels, or by food/outlay ratios - according to the data situation. The distinction also corresponds to distinct food behaviour. As outlay and income rise, ultra-poor (but not moderately poor) households maintain food/outlay and cereal/calorie ratios, thus revealing their "top priority" for more calories.

To that problem, avoidable intra-household food maldistribution usually contributes little. Seasonal, yearly and life-cycle variation, however, makes it worse.

Those at nutritional risk are fewer and poorer than is generally believed. By concentrating on these ultra-poor, programs to raise caloric intake can end such risk at reasonable cost and speed. Diffusing such programs to the moderately-poor diverts resources, both from their prime needs (schools, land, etc.) and from ultra-poor people's nutrition. More generally, most "poverty projects" - while reaching the moderately poor - will continue to bypass ultra-poor people, until their caloric status suffices for them to participate.

ACKNOWLEDGEMENTS

Many economists and natural scientists have patiently tried to help with comments, criticisms, and references to research. None should be blamed for any opinions or errors in my text. Indeed, I have tried to assess consumers' behavior - and planning priorities - so as to reach a clear position, on largely _economic_ grounds, in areas of _scientific_ controversy. Especially as I am not a natural scientist, this is a dangerous procedure; and I apologise to any persons listed below (especially the nutritionists) who may feel I have incompetently rejected, or incautiously over-interpreted, expert assistance freely given.

For that assistance I am deeply grateful. No comments were ignored; but to have accepted every comment would have produced an anodyne "on the one hand, on the other hand" paper, useless for policy-makers. At least, I hope this paper (a) clearly states an internally consistent set of positions, (b) presents a fair reading of the evidence, and (c) avoids bias. Indeed, my own preconceptions on some of the key issues (e.g. proportions below a nutrition-linked "poverty line"; continuity vs. threshold in nutritional risk; intra-household food discrimination; urban undernutrition) were the exact opposite of the conclusions to which a review of the evidence has led me.

I gratefully acknowledge help from Drs. George Beaton, Alan Berg, Robert Cassen, Angus Deaton, John Evans, Paul Isenman, Emanuel de Kadt, Derek Miller, Graham Pyatt, Shlomo Reutlinger, Daniel Roncari, Nevin Scrimshaw, Amartya Sen, Hans Singer, Inderjit Singh, Carl Taylor and Charles Taylor.

TABLE OF CONTENTS

Page No.

POVERTY, UNDERNUTRITION AND HUNGER

I. GENERAL INTRODUCTION

(a) Origins

In 1982, a Bank-wide Task Force reported on the impact of Bank activities on poor people. It showed that the proportion of the Bank's lending directed mainly at people in absolute or relative poverty had risen sharply - from about 5% in 1968 to 30% in 1980. Moreover, such activities showed rates of return at least as good as conventional lending, and succeeded, as intended, in benefiting mainly the poor. However, "neither borrowers nor lenders have been very effective in benefiting people who lack productive assets - the poorest 20%" (World Bank, 1982, pp. ii, 3, 5, 6-7). The report stressed the need for increasing the salience of poverty reduction in Bank "policy dialogue" with developing countries. But what can they learn from each other about appropriate policies for the poorest 20%?

While working with Alexander Shakow and Norman Hicks on the Secretariat of the Task Force, the author of the present paper was examining the characteristics of the poor and the poorest. This search was given special urgency by the Bank's partial success in raising the productivity of the poor, and its relative failure to do the same for the poorest. It may be, of course, that the "power structure" somehow prevents the poorest quintile of households in low-income countries - or the poorest decile in middle-income countries - from sharing the fruits of growth, while allowing moderately poor people to do so. Before accepting such a complicated hypothesis, however, we should look at the alternative: that very poor people (unlike the moderately poor) have characteristics that affect their capacity to benefit from development programs.

This is one of four linked Working Papers that aim to identify such characteristics, if any. The remaining three, "Labor and Poverty", "Demography and Poverty", and "The Assets of the Poor" will appear in 1983 or early 1984. Comments on all these papers are especially welcome, since it is intended to eventually revise and edit them for possible publication in book form.

(b) Data sources

It had been hoped to draw mainly on data sets for two ecologically comparable poor regions, one Asian and one African, each with micro-information from good village studies supported by regional data from larger sample surveys. Partly to follow data availability, partly to ensure that climatic fluctuations would permit study of variability as a poverty problem, we selected semi-arid areas in N.W. India and N. Nigeria. In N.W. India, main emphasis was to be placed on Rajasthan, Gujarat and Maharashtra; the first two States permit the use of village studies by the Agro-economic Research Center at Vallabh Vidyanagar, and the last two of Pravin Visaria's dis-aggregations of National Sample Survey data by household outlay-per-person deciles. In N. Nigeria, outstanding work at the Ahmadu Bello University (Department of Agricultural Economics) has produced three good surveys, each covering three villages (Patel, 1962; Vidyanagar and Vyas, 1969; Simmons, 1976 and 1976a).

As work progressed, however, it proved essential to support hypotheses from these sources with other enquiries, urban and rural, from a wide range of LDCs.

(c) Discontinuities

Not because this was originally expected or planned, but because of the accumulating evidence, the method of these Working Papers came increasingly to involve a search, not simply for relationships between poverty and other characteristics (e.g. participation rates, caloric inadequacy or family size), but for discontinuities in these relationships. It transpired that in LDCs such discontinuities usually occurred, not at the "poverty line" (i.e., not between the "poor" and the rest), but at a much lower level of income or outlay, per person or per consumer unit.

This is consistent with discontinuities observed in experimental work on producers' behavior. Notably, farmers exhibit "threshold" changes in behaviour (in respect of risk-aversion, reluctance to innovate, and - given the technology - reversal of the usual inverse relationship between size of operated farm and yield-per-acre) not around the "poverty-line", but around the much lower level of welfare at which subsistence appears to be endangered.

The "discontinuities" do not normally take the form of sudden, sharp rises or falls - as income or outlay, per person or per consumer unit, increases - in the proportion of persons within a given income or outlay interval. Rather there are reversals or intensifications - i.e., respectively, turning-points or points of inflexion - in behavior, as welfare changes around levels of great poverty. It is well-known that per-person income and outlay are usually distributed more or less lognormally. However, as these crude "welfare" indicators fall, adult female workforce participation rates increase until a "welfare" level signifying extreme poverty is reached - and then decrease with further falls in welfare. Ratios of food spending to total outlay, around much the same point on the "welfare" scale, shift from steady rises as poverty increases, to a more or less constant 80-85% level. Unemployment rates, a steadily increasing function of poverty, increase more sharply at very low income levels, and become more seasonally-unstable.

(d) Causality

On such issues, and generally, these Working Papers try to remain agnostic about causality. For example, we find that income-per-person, and other welfare indicators, tend to increase fairly steadily as household size falls, yet paradoxically also tend to be higher among groups of households with higher wealth or status. In seeking to reconcile these two findings we try not to make our explanations dependent upon whether large family size is cause or effect of (a) higher status or asset ownership, and/or (b) smaller welfare at a given status or wealth level. Perhaps larger households get poorer, as Malthus posited; perhaps poorer households are driven to get larger, as is averred by economic demographers of both Marxist and neo-classical persuasions.

The scarce and scattered data, the extreme rarity of time-series, and our ignorance of how very poor people reach decisions all suggest that one should defer attempts to make strong causal statements. These papers "explore the space" relating poverty to, say, economic and demographic characteristics. We must discover the direction and strength of the relationships, the gaps in observations on variables, and the turning-points or points of inflexion. Only then can we make sensible claims about causal directions. The author is too interested in policy inferences (and too incautious) to abjure all causal hypothesising. However, the preferrred form of conclusion should usually, at this stage, be neutral between "A causes B", "B causes A", and "C causes A and B". These papers are a first shot at outlining the shape, under different circumstances, of functional relations between poverty-variables (A) and characteristics-variables (B). Causal specification is largely left for others.

(e) Policy for a non-underclass

What, if any, policy conclusions can be drawn from causally inexplicit relationships? The answer depends on the nature, alterability, and costs of remedying the characteristics associated with moderate and extreme poverty. In particular, is remedying those characteristics likely to enable an affected person significantly to improve his or her level of welfare in a self-sustained way? Or is such improvement, instead, the likeliest way to remedy them? The answer to that question is logically independent of whether the characteristics "caused" the poverty level in the first place, or were caused by it.

Hence we can identify important policy implications of the "characteristics-poverty-ultrapoverty" links - implications independent of the causality of these links. One such implication is central to our whole enquiry. We find that the ultra-poor have very different behavioral characteristics from other poor (and nonpoor) people. Do these characteristics mean that most of the ultra-poor belong to an "underclass"?

It has been argued that the poorest 5-15 per cent of people in developed countries have "underclass" characteristics rendering it impossible, or prohibitively costly, to enable them to raise their income and productivity in a self-sustained way. These characteristics may be linked to misfortune (e.g. persistent mental deficiency in persons recently released from hospitals), to earlier choice (e.g. alcoholism), or even to demographic circumstance (e.g. widowed and childless status). Whatever the moral issues, and whether the characteristics cause poverty or are caused by it, the result is the same: the "underclass" cannot at reasonable cost be helped to help itself out of poverty, but must rely on social-security payments or on charity.

The evidence of these Working Papers strongly indicates that the great majority of the ultra-poor in LDCs are not, in this sense, an unreachable "underclass". Their extreme poverty is associated with lack of promising human and physical assets; with weak labor-market positions; with large families, high dependency ratios, and very high infant mortality; and with significant risks of nutritional damage. Only tiny proportions of the Third World's ultra-poor could survive as drug addicts, alcoholics, mental defectives, or even single-member families. These ultra-poor are mostly a resource, not a burdensome underclass.

This raises a second policy issue, also largely independent of the causal links between characteristics and ultra-poverty. Does an ultra-poor group require different projects and policies, to achieve self-sustained improvements in income and productivity, from those required by the moderately poor? These working papers suggest that "food and health first", especially for children - and policies to improve capacity to contest labor and asset markets - may be necessary preconditions for improved productivity for the ultra-poor. Otherwise, benefits from "poor people's projects" will continue to stop at the second quintile.

POVERTY, UNDERNUTRITION AND HUNGER

II.   CALORIES AND POVERTY

(a) Needed: a scalar measure of poverty

Are development efforts raising the productivity and welfare of the poor? To answer that, one must know who is poor. Nevertheless, poverty measurement is seldom a major concern for the allocator of a resource that produces mainly one clearly-defined good or service. A planner locating ten new primary schools, and satisfied that efficiency (cost-per-place, children's capacity to benefit) are satisfactory and similar in all locations, can equitably put the schools where most people are most severely 1/ deprived of the direct product, school places. He seldom feels the need to know how many of those people are poor. 2/

Most projects and programs, however, allocate resources with a whole range of products. An irrigation project leads to many different outputs, jobs, and social changes. If, once more, efficiency is adequate and similar in all locations, 3/ an "equitable" planner could well 4/ locate the project where its (given) net social return reduces poverty most.

But where is that? To decide, a measure of poverty is needed. It is also needed to compare past performance, in reducing poverty, of projects, policies, regions, or (e.g. when allocating aid) countries. There is widespread agreement that a person is in absolute primary 5/ poverty if and only if, and to the extent that, his or her resources are too few to meet "basic needs" by any combination of exchange (e.g. sale of labor-power for wages to buy food and shelter) and use (e.g. consumption of home-grown food).

But where is the borderline, the standard of poverty? Economists tend to define, as a "poverty line" some threshold level of private income, per person or per adult-equivalent (consumer unit, CU). 6/ This is associated with either observed or possible satisfaction of a set of levels of consumption. Households at poverty line income of course divide it in very different ways; but economists assume that people and households, especially if dangerously near such a poverty line, correctly perceive their needs and divide resources sensibly among them. Having set one income-per-CU threshold, economists can build in rural-urban, regional, international, or other variations in the poverty line - i.e. the level of personal income needed to avoid poverty - due to differences in access to borrowing, dissaving, and publicly provided commodities, and in the levels of, need for, and relative price of "basics" (Ahluwalia, et al., 1979).

Nevertheless, income or outlay, per person or per CU, is often badly estimated, especially for the poor. Where estimated, it is hard to compare across countries or regions. Where this is done, it relates to national or regional levels of satisfaction of "basic needs" (World Bank, World Development Report 1980 [hereafter WDR 1980], pp. 36, 40; Isenman, 1982) in an imperfect, non-linear, and unstable way (Hicks, 1982). Indeed, part of the interest of Sri Lanka (or Libya) is that basic needs are so much better (or worse) fulfilled than real income-per-person would suggest on the basis of cross-section regression (Sen, 1980, pp. 11-53).

Economists know that a given level of real GNP, or of real household income, per person or per CU in a region is not sufficient to infer the degree to which persons in that region fulfil their needs. Hence, to explain the Libyas and Sri Lankas, economists try to allow for inter-area differences in (a) income distribution, (b) relative prices and composition of the bundles of "needed" commodities, 7/ (c) availability of socially provided requirements such as health care, (d) gaps between received and disposable household income - transfers, and such constraining obligations as interest payments, rents, and perhaps some addictive forms of consumption. 8/ Thus economists have tended to move towards identifying a poverty borderline on a scale of "household resources, per CU, disposable for real consumption", instead of "GNP, or household, income per CU".

Yet even countries or regions with, at any appropriate exchange rates (Kravis et al., 1982), similar total values and distributions of private and public consumption per CU show very different proportions of households and persons in need. Kerala shows this by illustrating the converse. Kerala has far lower incidences of infant and child mortality, far higher life expectancy, and far less severe undernutrition - as compared with other Indian States - than relative real per-person or per-CU output, income, or consumption would lead us to expect. It used to be thought that Kerala's greater success in meeting health needs was due largely to its more equal income-distribution. Recently, however, attention has been drawn to Kerala's low absolute level of caloric intake per consumer (Soman, 1982) and to the large excess of mortality in Kerala's highland regions (with no obvious differences in income-distribution) (Ruzicka, 1982, p. 21). Better distribution clearly explains only part, perhaps a small part, of Kerala's good health (and low incidence of under-nutrition) for its given level of output, income or consumption per CU. At least as important are (a) composition of private and social products, especially their inclusion respectively of unusually widespread health services (Mencher, 1980) and cheap rootcrop foods (especially tapioca) (ibid.) - features less marked in the less "healthy" highland areas; (b) climatic factors, especially in the coastal lowlands, lowering nutritional requirements per person, as compared to North India (Sukhatme, 1982, p. 10; see below, pp. 12-14).

Such non-correspondences between household real income per CU and satisfaction of needs create a problem for economists. While ready to accept that high regional average real income does not ensure satisfaction of needs, they rightly cling to the assumption of rationality, and resist attributing poverty to "incorrect" household deployment of resources adequate to meet needs. Therefore - and because of the cost, difficulty, unreliability, instability and sometimes absurdity of comparisons (and sometimes even measurements) of real income and consumption - its adequacy to purchase a bundle of "needs" is becoming a less popular indicator of absolute poverty. Essentially, the search for alternatives arises because - due to non-comparabilities in composition of outlay - apparently identical real household income or outlay per CU, at any plausible exchange-rates, can in different places and times, reflect very different capacities to meet basic needs. Four other ways to identify the poor have been proposed.

The first is to abandon "absolute poverty" in favour of "relative poverty". On such a reading, "the poor" are those whose income or outlay falls below some proportion, say 30% of a society's average. However, the "proportion", and the borders of the "society" - village, sector, country, world - are completely arbitrary, as is the use of "average" rather than, say, median or mode. Removal of absolute need is incomparably more important than, say, enriching those below 30% of average income in Palm Beach. Inequality and poverty are different evils, not to be conflated by an index termed "relative poverty".

The second way of identifying "the poor" is as those who fail to reach critical levels of consumption in one or more elements of a vector of basic needs. This, too, is a retrograde step. It encourages users of the definition - contrary to the designers' intention - to confuse resource insufficiency with consumer inefficiency, to overestimate the latter, and thus to overestimate the chance of reducing "poverty" by persuading consumers to reallocate outlays. It involves setting arbitrary poverty cut-off points for each element in the vector - perhaps distinct levels for children and adults, for "poverty" and "destitution", for absolute and relative poverty, etc. Moreover, the old outlay-per-CU criterion at least allowed for households' different, probably correct, perception of needs; but any outsider seems free to add, deduct, or weight, as he wishes, components of a "basic needs" vector. This could produce chaos in any effort to locate and reduce poverty.

The third attempt to identify the poor is through some index of overall need satisfaction, such as the "physical quality of life" (PQLI) index (Morris, 1979). This measures, for any region, as a proportion of some optimal attainable level, (a) one-third of life expectancy at age 1, plus (b) one-third of survival chances from birth to age 1, plus (c) one-third of adult literacy rate. Each of these three indicators (unlike GNP, which in principle can be checked by income, output, or expenditure) has at most one, usually bad, measure in most LDCs. As to "one-third each", the equal weights give no more than an illusion of avoiding "an uncomfortable index-number problem" (Shah, 1979, p. 7). The PQLI has the advantage of measuring results rather than inputs - health and literacy rather than doctors and teachers (or their salaries, which are what GNP includes). But there is no reason why all, and only, those three indicators should be in the PQLI; why all three are equally important; or why there should exist any cut-off value for PQLI to indicate absolute poverty. The welfare corresponding to any given value of PQLI (including any proposed cut-off) would, incidentally, vary greatly with the age-structure of the population. It is infeasible to use a PQLI for any purposes of assessment or allocation; such an index is arbitrary.

The fourth approach is followed here. We seek the level of income and/or outlay which - allowing for prices - enables its recipient to meet just one basic need. If this proves possible, we shall be able to identify the poor (and to examine their characteristics) in one of three ways, with the choice depending largely on data availability. We can measure outlay or income; or physical indicators of fulfilment of the need in question (e.g. caloric adequacy); or the proportion of outlay or income used to fulfil the need - the proportion will, in poverty, tend to exceed some (rather high) figure. The numbers, and a large majority of the persons, identified by all three methods should be similar.

For this approach to succeed, fulfilment of the "key" need must be closely related to income or outlay per person. It must also be related closely to, or must be met as a necessary condition for, meeting other needs. And it must possess a definable "adequate level". We can then establish how far how many people - in a village, country, social group, etc. - fall below such an indicator, how severely, 9/ for how long, 10/ with what consequences, and with what costs of remedy.

(b) <u>The case for a food adequacy standard (FAS)</u>

We shall define "moderately poor" and "ultra-poor" by food adequacy. About 20% appears empirically to be a more or less irreducible minimum of income or outlay (which seldom differ much, for long, among very poor people 11/) spent on non-food. Income or outlay, just sufficient on this assumption to command the average caloric requirement for one's age, sex and activity group (ASAG) in a given climatic and work environment, will be taken as meeting the poverty FAS; this is income or outlay on the borderline of <u>poverty</u>, indicating a <u>risk of hunger</u>. Income or outlay, just sufficient to command 80% of this average requirement, will be taken as meeting the ultra-poverty FAS; this is income or outlay at the borderline between poverty and <u>ultra-poverty</u>, indicating a <u>risk of undernutrition</u> and a severe risk of important anthropometric shortfalls 12/ (see below, pp. 14-19).

It is not just the ultra-poor who constitute the poverty problem. The moderately poor, apart from being unable to meet many non-food needs, can also be very hungry at times: hungry to the point of lethargy, even pain. However, only the ultra-poor suffer, on account of poverty, serious health hazards on account of dietary underfulfilment. Conversely the moderately poor usually reveal by behavior, 13/, and constitute for the planner, principally a problem in asset ownership, education, etc., rather than in acute food need.

However we define food adequacy, a FAS would indicate the level of income or outlay (including the value of self-consumed output) required by a person to meet "normal" food requirements, at the full average level for the "poverty" FAS, at the 80% level for the ultra-poverty FAS. In adults, these requirements are for work, basal metabolic rate, tissue replacement and disease protection (Durnin and Passmore, 1967). In children, requirements for adequate growth, and probably for the play required for adequate development, must be added. In women of child-bearing age, probabilities of pregnancy and lactation must be allowed for.

Income (or outlay) sufficient to obtain enough food to avoid (a) undernourishment and (b) hunger, are appealing tests for the absence, respectively, of (a) extreme poverty and (b) moderate poverty. Adequate food is necessary to enjoy fully other benefits and rights. 14/ Income and outlay levels, just sufficient to avoid (a) undernutrition or (b) hunger, turn out to be associated with spending behavior in moderately stable and hence predictable ways. 15/ A definition of poverty in food terms - a FAS - is also attractive intuitively, because the poorest quintile of persons in an LDC seldom spend less than two-thirds of income on food, and usually spend most of their working time in producing or processing it. Various forms of FAS underlie efforts to define and track "poverty lines", from their origins in the Rowntree-Booth studies to the recent work of scholars in developing countries and international organisations (Ahluwalia, Carter and Chenery, 1979; Dandekar and Rath, 1971; Srinivasan and Bardhan, 1974).

A FAS does not imply a single treatment for poverty, such as the provision of more cash, or of more calories per unit of cash. Indeed, the most cost-effective approach, to getting people above the level of income or outlay that meets their FAS, is frequently to reduce requirements, not to raise intake. Fewer "secret sharers" of food, viz. unwanted parasites or gut bacteria; better timing or composition of food intakes; fewer pregnancies producing children who die after a short period of hungry life; shorter walks (at 80-100 calories per mile) to, from and among workplaces and water sources: the means to improved fulfilment of FAS can involve action on a wide range of basic-needs fronts. These may be easier or cheaper, per person brought to a FAS, than increases in dietary intake.

Does a household's income or outlay, given the non-food needs of its members (see p. 40) suffice to bring its members enough food _relative to requirements_? That is the best single indicator of whether those persons are poor. Daily requirements, however, vary greatly among persons, between places and seasons, and even for a particular person from day to day. So do food prices and availabilities. To the extent that people can without damage _adjust_ requirements to availabilities, by varying work done or metabolic efficiency, fluctuations in average intake may well cut average requirements (pp. 31-33), yet may also increase the risk of _periodic_ deprivation. In any period, a ratio of at least 75-80% between food expenditure and total expenditure in a household appears to be a necessary, but not sufficient, condition of likely shortfall below FAS in most countries (p. 40).

(c) _Calories provide the best poverty-related FAS_

Poverty is not the same as undernutrition, and neither is it the same as hunger. However, "undernourished because poor" and "hungry because poor (though not undernourished)" are attractive _indicators_ of income or outlay levels needed to escape poverty. However, such FASs will not give the desired scalar poverty-indicator, unless a single measure of food adequacy can be found. A caloric indicator is best. Although a few people receive too few dietary calories despite high incomes and outlays, and a few receive enough despite exceptionally low incomes and outlays, the vast majority of hungry or undernourished people are receiving too few calories because they are poor. Very few non-poor people are hungry or undernourished. And shortfalls in nutrients other than calories are almost always _either_ due to inadequate caloric intake, _or_ neither related to nor cost-effectively relieved by general income increases.

Protein deficiency is almost always cured once caloric needs are met. In seven Indian states in 1975, of rural households receiving inadequate protein, the proportion receiving enough calories ranged from zero (in four states) to 6.0%. 16/ Since then, protein requirements estimates have been scaled down further (Poleman, 1981, p. 12; Ebrahim, 1979, pp. 63-4). The great majority of people who do not meet them will do so if each food they now eat is increased until they get enough calories; this (or even, in many cases, just adding empty calories) will "free", for appropriate uses, sufficient proteins previously used for energy purposes. Except in some root-crop cultures, and in a few cases involving bulky weaning food, very few people are protein-malnourished except as a result of caloric under-nourishment. 17/ The great majority of nutritionists now see shortage of dietary energy as the real problem, and speak of "the great protein fiasco" as a diversion from its solution (McLaren, 1974, p. 93). Protein deficiency is rare among people whose income suffices to obtain enough calories (Miller, 1979, p. 201).

Protein imbalance - wrong ratios among amino-acids, leading to incapacity to utilise, to an adequate level, an otherwise sufficient protein intake - is probably even rarer as an _independent_ condition in those with enough calories. Even low-cost dietary variation, such as adding pulses to a cereal diet, usually suffices to prevent deficiency in a particular amino-acid. Moreover, work among moderately undernourished adults (landless laborers in Maharashtra) suggests that they develop special biosynthetic capacities to maintain, in red-cell and plasma protein, amino-acids deficient in their food, and thus to avoid deficiency diseases. 18/ Higher birth-weight, i.e. more energy intake (not more or better-balanced proteins) for pregnant women, appears to help such biosynthesis (Ebrahim, 1979, pp.63-4).

Deficiencies of vitamins, iron, magnesium, iodine and other micro-
nutrients occur on a large scale even without caloric shortage. Cures,
however, are likely to be achieved most cost-effectively, not by measures
to raise income - or otherwise to raise intake (or cut requirements) of some
or all foods - but by public action such as fortification of salt with
iodine or vitamin A. The per-person cost of such action is negligible
(Berg, 1973).

Apart from calories, therefore, nutrients can be divided into
two groups. For some, inadequate intake is most cost-effectively cured by
making caloric intake adequate. For others, social rather than private
nutritional action is appropriate. Hence there are very few cases in which
private action, other than action to increase caloric intake or reduce
calorie requirements, is likely to cost-effectively bring people above the
minimum necessary standard. In most such cases, e.g. increased vitamin C
consumption to prevent scurvy, small and low-cost (or zero-cost) dietary
changes will help. Therefore, it is reasonable in the great majority of
cases to equate a "food adequacy standard", attainable by reduction of
personal poverty, to a caloric adequacy standard.

We shall then be measuring as convenient - and seeking policies
to reduce - the numbers with, and severity of, (i) income, or outlay, per
CU shortfalls below the level required to meet the caloric standard; or
(ii) shortfalls below that standard itself, indicated by dietary, anthropometric, or clinical measurement; or (iii) cases where there is need to
allocate more than some set "critical" proportion of income or outlay to
meet that caloric standard. Both the standard and the outlay needed to
meet it can vary across space and time, but the indicators of numbers in
and severity of shortfall - the indicators of poverty - should remain comparable, consistent and stable. The problems outlined on pp. 4-5 should
be solved by defining such a caloric standard. But what should it be?

(d) Current caloric standards overstate even average "Western" requirements

Between 1955 and 1971, the FAO/WHO dietary energy requirements
(DER) at 10°C for the average reference man (weighing 65kg.) were reduced
from 3200 kcals per day to 3000, and for the average reference woman (55kg.)
from 2300 to 2200. ("Reference" persons are aged 20-39, healthy, moderately
active for 8 hours daily, lightly active for 4-6 hours, active in recreation
or household duties for 2, and in bed for 8.) FAO/WHO requirements for
older persons were reduced more than proportionately (FAO, 1973, p. 28-31;
Poleman, 1981, p. 9).

Subsequent work has drastically scaled down these average "Western"
DERs. For persons aged 23-50 and moderately active, the 1980 US Food and
Nutrition Board DER was 38.6 kcals/kg/day (19.7% below the FAO/WHO 1973
figure) for men, and 36.4 (9.1% below) for women. 19/ The US Department of
Health, Education and Welfare (DHEW), allowing for the fact that weight gain
after the age of 29 is almost entirely superfluous fat, estimates age-
specific kcal/kg requirements for growth to median US weight aged 20-29,
and for weight maintenance thereafter; results are even further below
FAO/WHO 1973 standards, e.g. 21% below for men and women aged 30-39; and 15%
for men, and 20% for women, aged 50-59 (DHEW, 1979, and FAO/WHO, 1973,
p. 32). Even these DHEW standards are too high, for two reasons. First,
they assume that the total actual weight of the median US citizen at age
20-29 is desirably attained, and later maintained, by caloric intake - i.e.
includes no excess fat. Second, the DHEW standards ignore the loss with
ageing of lean cell mass (i.e. of mass requiring food); 20/ hence requirements
for older people are particularly overstated. 21/

We can confirm that DHEW's requirements are still too high, by matching them against intake data from its 1971-4 Health and Nutrition Evaluation Survey (HANES). In HANES, the 50th percentile of men got 2225 kcals/day or 85.7% of supposed DERs, and of women 1527 kcals/day (86.6%). Of the 1657 examined men over 65, over half were 30% or more below the DHEW's DERs, and 1 in 10 were 60% or more below! 22/

The use of one-day recall means that (1) HANES's reported intakes (while substantially accurate) somewhat exceed true intakes at the lower levels. 23/ Moreover, although target body weights may have been set some-what too low, most US persons exceed even revised targets (Andres, 1981, esp. pp. 493-4); obesity is widespread, and (outside drug-addicted families) caloric inadequacy is clinically almost absent, in the USA. Therefore (2) true intakes generally exceed DERs. Yet (3) HANES intakes at most levels are well below DHEW requirements. From (1), (2) and (3), it follows that (4) DHEW requirements, although 15-20% below FAO/WHO levels, still substantially overstate true average DERs.

A further source of overstatement in some estimates of DERs is that they are "safe", i.e. above average DER (DHEW, 1979, p. 2; FAO/WHO, 1973, p. 24; Sukhatme, 1977; but cf. FAO, 1974, p. 2; Srinivasan, 1980, pp. 1-2). Other estimates, while correct for average person-days, are above the needs (and in-takes) of many people with low basal metabolic rates (BMRs) or high work efficiency (pp. 26-31). As FAO/WHO makes clear (FAO/WHO, 1973, p. 10) this could lead to overestimates of numbers below true DER, if below-average intake normally goes together with below-average DER.

The FAO/WHO/UNU committee, currently reviewing DERs, is being pressed to distinguish "physiological energy need" (to maintain body weight and health) from the higher "recommended energy allowance" (to discharge full economic functions well) (Taylor and Beaton, 1980, pp. 10-11). Presumably the FAO/WHO 1973 DERs for "moderate activity" fall somewhere between these two concepts. Informal enquiries, however, suggest that much, probably most, expert opinion would now follow the DHEW and other evidence for an average DER for Western "reference man" at least 20% below the FAO/WHO 1973 level, i.e. 25% below the FAO 1957 level. And even a 10% reduction in DERs typically cuts, by over a quarter, the proportions estimated to be under-nourished - too poor to afford their DER - in a country (Reutlinger and Alderman, 1980, p. 15).

Before asking how such DERs - and the implicit poverty-line incomes needed to afford them - have to be adapted to (i) tropical LDCs (pp. 12-14) and (ii) inter- and intrapersonal variability in DERs, there are two prior issues. Has the use of FAO/WHO averages, even with minimal adaptation, modified their propensity to overstate true DERs? Are there special circumstances of human life that alter the degree of overstatement? The answers could somewhat alter our measure of poverty-line income, and hence greatly 24/ alter estimates of the numbers and intensity of shortfall.

*   *   *

The use of these averages has further exaggerated the numbers too poor to afford DERs, in three ways. First, despite FAO/WHO's warning, their 1973 estimates have often been used as measuring DERs of every person on every day. Yet many person-days on which below-average requirements are eaten are days when requirements are in fact below average. 25/

Second, the time-lag in analysis and publication means that several studies used pre-1973, and thus even higher, FAO caloric require- ments. An excellent study in Nigeria used 1957 data, was carried out in 1971, published in 1976, and in 1980 was incorporated into internationally distri- buted (over)estimates of the numbers of Nigerians too poor to eat properly! (Simmons, 1976, pp. 9, 36; Stewart, 1980, p. 16).

Third, important local sets of guidelines, perhaps in the interests of erring on the safe side, 26/, further inflate DERs. For example, the Indian Council for Medical Research in 1980 reissued, substantially unrevised, its 1968 DERs (presumably based on the 1957 FAO averages). The average Indian male sedentary worker, apparently weighing 49.1 kgs and taken as ICMR's "consumption unit", was estimated to require 2,400 kcal/day, as against 2063 in FAO/WHO (1973), and at most 1930 for the (still inadequately scaled down) US 1980 measure. 27/ For other groups of male workers, and for women, DERs are proportionately even further above FAO/WHO levels. 28/ As if to confirm the overstatement, Indian female athletes, plainly in good health and choosing exceptionally high levels of energy use (and intake?), fall well short of ICMR caloric intakes recommended for their sedentary counterparts. 29/

*   *   *

Two "special circumstances" may be prone to over-high caloric allowances even under Western conditions (and are more prevalent in LDCs than in the West): heavy work and pregnancy. The problem with heavy work requirements is not with the FAO/WHO data, but with "translations" in current use. 30/ The problem with the requirements of pregnancy appears to be more serious.

FAO/WHO, "recognising that this [as a safe] recommendation differs from other estimates for energy that are average requirements, recommends 80,000 kcal for pregnancy" - exactly twice its previous recommendation (FAO/WHO, p. 35). However, Ebrahim points out that, inasmuch as "stunting in the mother" casuses higher infant death risks, it "cannot be overcome ... by a good diet in pregnancy"; and that - presumably, almost entirely for women originally not stunted - follow-up studies of famines (1944-5 in Holland, 1941-3 in Leningrad) reveal severe impact on birth-weights only with exposure in the second half of pregnancy. Moreover, of seven sets of national standards for a 280-day pregnancy, three (UK, Colombia, Guatemala) estimate requirements of 61,600 kcals as against FAO/WHO's 80,000 (the other four being 88,200 in India, 89,040, 109,760, and - for Canada in 1974 - an astonishing 141,120). Ebrahim implies that all these figures are much too high: "Studies on the energy costs of pregnancy indicate that about 100 calories per day extra are required for the entire gestation period ... 10 in the first trimester, 65 in the second and 220 in the third", or only 27,550 for the whole pregnancy, 31/ as against FAO/WHO's 80,000. This is for 55 kg reference women; if, as most accounts suggest, requirements are per maternal kg., they would be lower in LDCs, for example 21,050 in India (as against ICMR's 88,200). 32/

It would be very wrong to advise anything that increased risk of dangerously low birth-weight, which is strongly correlated with infant and child mortality. But diversion of scarce nutritional resources to pregnant women could also cost lives - if those resources did not significantly raise at-risk birthweight, or if that rise could be more cost-effectively obtained (e.g. by reducing the pregnant women's exposure to malaria). In view of Dr. Ebrahim's usual and justified caution it is striking - and convincing - that his data appear to imply an extra DER in pregnancy below 30,000 kcal. It casts further severe doubt on many high estimates of absolute nutritional deprivation, of numbers too poor to avoid it - and of intra-family bias in food distribution against pregnant women. 33/

(e) <u>Climate, weight, and other factors cut relative LDC calorie requirements</u>

Apart from the need to scale down Western average DERs, those of LDCs differ from Western levels. Factors lowering LDCs' relative DERs - climates, age-structures, body-weights - are slow to change. Factors increasing them - more infections and pregnancies, longer walks to harder work - more readily diminish with development, and/or are matters in which welfare is most cost-effectively increased, not by higher caloric intakes, but by attacking the immediate causes of higher requirements, e.g. waterborne parasites sharing human food. At present the age-structure, unemployment, and body-weight typical of most LDCs, and especially of their poor families, outweigh other factors and set DERs well below DC levels. Together with the factors discussed on pp. 25-34, this means that <u>numbers "too poor to avoid serious risk of undernutrition" are 10-15% of populations in, say, India or Nigeria, not 40-60% as often claimed; far more are moderately poor, but require in the first instance other remedies than more calories</u>, and income increases geared to other purposes than food. 34/

This is confirmed, in different ways, by three recent observations. The first is a decline in Chilean infant mortality rates from 251 per 1,000 in 1935 to 55 per 1,000 in 1975, despite the absence of any improvement in nutritional status - a development paralleled in other Latin American countries (Solimano and Vine, 1982, pp.96-106). The second is the World Food Survey's estimate that undernourished persons, allowing for variability in requirements, roughly equal the number of persons ingesting kcals below 1.2BMR (FAO, 1977, pp. 50-54) - a figure of only 1,770 kcals/day for Indian reference males at average body-weight (FAO/WHO, pp.107-8; and see also fns. 27-28) and correspondingly for other ASAGs, implying undernutrition at population level below 15 per cent. Third is the expert observation that not poverty-induced under-ingestion but "diarrhoeal diseases are the underlying cause of most endemic undernutrition in adults" (Nichols, 1978, p.1968).

We now consider the separate factors influencing ratios of requirements in LDCs to those in temperate Western countries.

1. Climate

DERs are lower in LDCs partly because DC reference levels assume a 10°C (50°F) mean environmental temperature. The 1950 and 1957 FAO Committee on Calorie Requirements "recommended a decrease by 5% for every 10°C of mean annual external temperature above" 10°C, i.e. by about 7½% for most of India and Nigeria. This was subsequently confirmed by evidence from measures of kcal metabolic rates in different areas of Japan (Suzuki et al., 1959), and of Papua New Guinea (Hipsley, 1969, p. 8). The 1973 FAO/WHO Committee, however, removed this decrease; it concluded that "there was no quantifiable basis for correcting the resting and exercise DERs according to the climate", partly because "clothes and housing [and] heating" may be used, instead of (food-energy-requiring) heat production by muscles, to maintain body temperature in cold climates; and partly because not <u>all</u> measurements in tropical communities confirm lower basal metabolic rates (FAO/WHO, 1973, pp. 27-8).

The logic of this amendment appears rather unconvincing. DERs for heat production clearly decline with the gap between outside temperature and normal body temperature; "in tropical coastal areas like Kerala external temperatures are close to body temperature, heat dissipation is negligible and body weight can be maintained at relatively lower intakes [of dietary

energy. In cold places, even with warm garments, persons dissipate body
heat through breathing and body-weight has to be maintained [by] higher
intakes" (Sukhatme, 1982, p.19). Normal body temperature in the tropics
is less than 1°C above temperate-zone levels, while outside temperature
averages 10-15°C or more. Therefore fewer food kcals are needed in hot
climates; one is not always indoors in cold ones.

        Other factors may reinforce this. First, in colder climates,
three independent factors - (normally) greater income-per-person, higher
availability of animal relative to vegetable calorie sources, and adaptive
effect of human tastes - may tend to raise the ratio of proteins and fats
to total dietary calories; this may well tend to raise the basic metabolic rate
(Hipsley, 1969, pp. 10-11, 13, 15). Second, selection of the non-shivering means
of thermogenesis - an active, respiration-increasing process involving
mobilization of brown fat - can further raise an animal's, including a
human's, dietary energy requirements in colder climates (Rothwell and
Stock, 1979, esp. p. 34; Nicholls, 1979, esp. pp. 1-2, 10, 17-18).

        It is therefore not surprising that an authoritative source, two
years after FAO/WHO (1973), concluded that usually BMRs are "some 10%
lower in the tropics" so that (while 5% per 10°C may be spuriously
accurate) "it seems sensible" - given basic biophysics, perhaps reflected
in common experience that heat cuts appetite - "to reduce the recommended
intakes ... by 5-10% where the mean annual temperature exceeds 25°C".
(Davidson et al., 1975, p.32) The evidence for lower tropical BMRs is
stronger than it looks, because many measurements on at-risk tropical
populations (e.g. impoverished farm laborers) - being made less than
fifteen hours after prolonged exertion - overstate BMRs considerably
(see below, fn. 63), thus understating downward adjustments to BMRs
caused by tropical conditions (or perhaps by successful genetic adaptation
to them: adaptive selection of survivors from a given gene pool, not changes in it).

        Two complications affect the downward impact of tropical heat
upon DERs and hence on income required to meet them. First, though
"tropicality" cuts DERs, Petrasek (1978) shows that acclimatization to it (at least
when combined with heavy exertion) can increase them. In other words,
for heavy exertion, acclimatized people in temperate conditions need fewer
calories than unacclimatized people in the tropics. Yet Petrasek also
confirms that, for given tasks, "in acclimatized subjects ... lower energy
expenditure [and] lower intake were found" in tropical conditions. 35/ It
is to such subjects that DERs, and implicit income needs, apply.

        Second, bodily fat requirements in tropical LDCs are a complex
issue, because human needs point in opposite directions. For coping
with humid heat, the problems of the needlessly fat person, cow or chicken
are familiar - and are seen in the tropical selection, natural or induced,
of cattle, etc., with genes making for low ratios of weight to surface area,
i.e. high sweating capacity, and low requirements to drag fat about, per
unit of muscle and hence per unit of (non-body) weight moved (Lee, 1957).
On this argument, people too, especially poor workpeople, in the tropics
should aim - within the safe range - at lower fat/weight ratios than in
temperate areas. On the other hand, the seasonal and year-to-year variations
in income - and, for the poor, in food availability - may give survival value
to the deposition of weight gain as fat, which is more easily and safely
"mobilized" than lean in emergencies when external food is scarce (Payne
and Dugdale, 1977; but compare Naismith et al. , 1982). However, since there
are alternative bodily responses to such emergencies - and since even
fat people lose about 40% of energy in mobilizing body stores as
against under 10% of typical losses in grain stores (Longhurst and
Payne, 1981, p. 10, 52) - the permanent biophysical drawbacks
of fat in the tropics could well outweigh its periodic advantages as a

reserve. If so, tropical DERs (and implicit income requirements) would
fall further. All this, however, is rather speculative!

2. Weight, height and standards

Body-weights are significantly lower, in most cases, in tropical
developing countries than for persons of similar age and sex in temperate
developed countries. Yet tropical DERs are commonly calculated for
reference, not actual, weight. For example, some female farmers in Upper
Volta were shown by a careful survey to average 50.6 kg. weight, 20% of it
fat; yet these adults, for whom extra weight would almost entirely mean
extra fat, were then assessed for caloric requirements at the FAO/WHO's
reference weight (for Western women) of 55 kg. (Bleiberg et al., 1980,
pp. 71, 74). Indian adult females appear to average 42 kg., yet DERs are
estimated at the ICMR's 45 kg. reference weight (see fns. 27, 28 on
actual weights). "The Indian reference man is an adult of 20-30 years of
age, weighing 55 kg." (Chakrabarti and Panda, 1981, p. 1275); since in
rural areas he actually averages about 49.1 kg. (see fn. 27) and since
adult calorie requirements are proportional to weight (FAO/WHO, 1973,
p. 31) this overestimates them by 10.7%. These are typical procedures,
even among first-class researchers.

The problem is especially acute in deciding how many people are
too poor (and by how much) to meet the average dietary energy requirements
for their age-sex-activity group. People who are supposed to be (and often
are) "too poor to eat enough" usually weigh much less, not merely than ICMR
or FAO references, but than national averages for their ASAG. 36/   Are
they, then, not so poor, because they have smaller bodies to feed? Clearly,
many researchers - in using standard Western body-weight to assess DERs
of persons weighing 10-20 per cent less - imply that low body weight, due
to low weight-for-height or to low height-for-age, is in itself harmful.

Obviously, there comes a point when this is correct - when small
is harmful. There seems, however, no reason to push extra fat - and almost
all food-induced weight gain after age 29 is fat - onto healthy adults.
This is confirmed - despite the easy misinterpretation that big is good -
by Indian evidence that higher lean weight improves adult working efficiency,
and that total weight and height predict this efficiency far worse than
does the habitual level of physical exertion (itself raising lean/fat
weight ratios) (NNMB, 1979, pp. 140-1). Even as early as age 13, extra
food does not cure early undernutrition, but "would lead to obesity ...
after the thirteenth birthday the recommended [calorie] intake should be
[in direct proportion to] body-weight ... as in adults" (FAO/WHO, 1973,
p. 34). If so, then, especially for poor and hence low-weight families,
the great mass of typical DERs - for persons aged above 13 - are further
overestimated by being directed to higher, reference weights, severely
inflating estimated numbers "too poor to eat enough" in the tropics. There
simply has to be something wrong with estimates implying that 69 per cent
of all Indians, to eat adequately, should raise intakes by a daily average
of 330-400 kcals (Reutlinger and Alderman, 1980) - 20 per cent of intake
for many of the adults involved; they would become poor and fat instead of
poor and lean. (See pp. 21-3 for the - surprisingly small - impact of pregnancy
on this.)

The case for using reference or target weights, rather than actual
weights, to set DERs - and thus for classifying (say) 40-70 per cent of
Indian households, rather than 10-15 per cent, as ultra-poor and therefore at
risk of undernourishment - must rest upon the children under 13.   There

is some doubt about whether extra household calories (due to extra income or otherwise) will do very much to raise children's weights near to target levels; 37/ but, leaving this important matter aside, the case for gearing DERs to children's Harvard "target weight" is based on three arguments: that assessing requirements merely by their actual, low height-for-age and weight-for-height would impair physical development, mental development, or survival prospects.

For extremely low-weight children, such arguments are plainly true. There are perhaps as many as 10-15% of Indian households too poor to feed their children adequately; up to 5% of "severely undernourished" children on Harvard anthropometric standards; and - presumably almost all from that high-risk group - about 2-4% of children with marasmus or (rarely) kwashiorkor when examined. Such severely underweight children need catch-up calories per "target" kg., not merely per kg. of their current, inadequate, weight. But the three arguments do not carry over to children with so-called mild or moderate undernutrition (MMU) - the majority of children supposed to come from households too poor to eat enough. Such children are poor: they need more schooling, cleaner water, better health care; their parents need more assets, more power. Such children are also probably quite often hungry. But such children are not poor-unto-undernourishment. Their hunger makes them unhappy, and is therefore bad. But it does not normally place them at hazard. More food for moderately poor children, unless accompanied by educational and health measures to encourage more creative activity as well, far from opening the doors of better school or work performance, is likelier to constitute "mapping into obesity" (Seckler, 1980).

(i) Child weight and height and later physical work

Do children with MMU need more weight-for-height (or height-for-age) to raise their adult physical work performance? In rural Hyderabad in 1977, male adolescent physical work capacity aged 14-17 (AWC) was compared with recorded child height retardation aged five (CHR). Among 42 sedentary youths, no systematic AWC trends were seen as between the seven who had no or normal CHR (zero to two S.D.s below standard), the 10 with mild CHR (two to three S.D.s below), and the 12 with moderate CHR (three to four S.D.s); but these 29 together averaged 31.0% higher AWC than the other 14 sedentary youths, who had suffered severe CHR (over four S.D.s below the standard for five-year-olds). Among 54 physically active youths, the 21 who had suffered "mild" CHR showed subsequent AWC 10.8% below the twelve "normals", but not significantly different from the 16 "moderates"; these 49 together averaged 50.0% higher AWC than the other five active youths, who had suffered severe CHR. 38/

The apparent policy conclusions from these striking results for severe CHR, and the weak and ambiguous results for less severe states, is clear: to improve physical work performance in later life, concentrate, in improving nutrition for under-fives, on those with severe anthropometric retardation. This conclusion is strengthened by several other bits of evidence.

First, a given amount more food at ages 0-5 can do most to increase mature height, and hence AWC, among the severely underfed. In all persons in a given population group, barely half the variance in anthropometry is linked to nutritional history. (The rest is due to illness, or else is genetic: Sukhatme, 1981, p.6). Among the truncated group of adolescents excluding those who had suffered severe CHR, there is less variance to explain or remedy, and common sense suggests that the relative role of childhood diet was smaller.

Second, "over 70% of energy intake for children is used for maintenance, a variable but significant percentage for activity, and only a small proportion for growth". Hence "when DERs are marginally adequate, growth and weight gain may be curtailed, but activity is more likely to be sacrificed to maintain some growth" (Graham et al., 1981, p. 551) Therefore, more dietary calories for under-fives with MMU probably serve mainly to increase childhood activity. This is a worthy goal, but less important (to the childhood determination of adult "ceilings" of work capacity) than extra calories, and hence increased growth, for under-fives with severe CHR. (Nor is the extra play often essential for psychomotor development: see fn. 81).

Third, while heights at ages 5 and 15 are strongly correlated (NIN, 1978) - due to both genes and early feeding - less-than-severe CHR harms AWC much less than do low levels of adolescent physical activity. 39/ Correspondingly, the effect on AWC of MMU in childhood, even if it does produce irreversible height shortfalls, can to some extent be overcome in adults by combining weight gain (to build up weight-for-height) with higher activity levels (to build muscle size and tone). Severe CHR (normally itself due in part to undernutrition) cannot be fully made up later. 40/

Some 80-90% of children, counted as undernourished in five national nutrition surveys, had adequate weight-for-height. Yet in adolescents and adults, provided weight-for-height is adequate, low height-for-age (except at extremes) probably offers few disadvantages (Seckler, pp.1-3, 7-11 and Tables 1,2). In 57 Indian men aged 20-35, daily productivity in wire-bundling was unrelated to height, provided either weight or lean weight was held constant. 41/

Finally, there is some recent evidence that current intake of dietary energy, not childhood anthropometric status, most influences current physical productivity. This, at least, is one interpretation authoritatively offered for the above results from India. 42/ This suggests that most of the impact of mild and moderate childhood undernutrition on adult work performance can be made good later. 43/

(ii) Undernutrition and mental development

Impact of diet on physical work performance, then, does not provide a strong case for the present practice of raising childhood or other weights, requiring caloric support, from actual levels towards significantly higher local "norms", let alone to Western levels - except in kwashiorkor or marasmus, or when actual heights or weights of children indicate severe malnutrition or faltering. Nor, therefore, does "physical productivity of calories" justify the currently high estimates of (a) poverty-line income (needed to afford enough food to maintain such over-high target weights), or therefore (b) numbers undernourished-because-poor, i.e. below these incorrect "poverty lines". Least of all does the effect of extra calories, in remedying the impact on physical work performance of MMU, warrant attacking MMU with anything approaching the urgency justified for severe states. What of the argument that such urgency is, however, justified even for MMU because early undernourishment retards mental performance?

Severe deprivation of calories, and probably of proteins, does so in laboratory animals, and almost certainly in human infants exposed to severe marasmus (though some still argue that in humans the effect may be reversible) (Brozek, 1977; DHEW, 1979; Berg, 1981, pp. 10-11). However, once again,

MMU - caloric shortfall leading (say) to weight/age ratios of 60-90% of
Gomez standards - does not seem to have similar effects, scaled-down or
otherwise, on mental performance. Once again, the case for describing
as "undernourished because poor" one whose income does not suffice to
buy enough food to avoid MMU is not made out. Indeed, more schooling -
and parental income, leisure, and even perhaps power - is a securer route
to mental performance (and more generally to a decent life) than more
calories.

The most systematic and careful attempt to relate MMU to mental
performance is that of Klein, Freeman and their colleagues at INCAP.
Guatemalan children, some suffering from MMU (but almost none severely
underfed), were divided into three groups: one given calorie supplementation,
one calories-plus-protein, and one nothing. Pregnant and lactating women
were also supported, nutritionally and medically, in various ways.
Anthropometric, caloric and mental performance measures have now been made
for over seven years on many of these children. The most recent account
of the results (Klein, 1981) clearly shows that:

- Even at early ages, anthropometric indicators - in the range
between normality and MMU - show extremely weak relationships with scores
on eleven "psychological tests" (digit memory, verbal inference, block
designs, etc.). At age 7, linear regressions of eleven such indicators
upon two anthropometric measures (head circumference and height),
plus sex, and on two good indicators or socio-economic status - house quality
and maternal characteristics - showed r^2 insignificant in five cases,
0.5-0.8 in four, and 0.11 in two. β-coefficients on anthropometric variables
are not available (Klein, 1981, pp. 35-42; Freeman et al., 1980, p. 1282).

- Even this very weak impact of anthropometric indicators on
"psychological test performance" cannot be wholly or even mainly attributed
to different nutrition, because they embody not only nutritional history
but also the influences of illness and genetic endowment (Freeman, p. 1279;
Klein et al., 1972, p. 221).

- At age 7, the independent impact of earlier or current MMU as
measured by anthropometric indicators - though not that of quality of
home, or of parental contacts - on "school performance" (unlike that on
psychological test performance) is not significantly different from zero
(Klein, 1981, pp. 45, 54, 86-7).

(iii) Undernutrition, illness and death

Here too, an important recent study - by Chen and his colleagues
in rural Bangladesh - indicates that MMU at ages 0-5 has no statistically
discernible effect on infant or child mortality rates, but that "severe"
undernutrition raises these rates substantially. 2019 children aged
12-23 months were classified according to the Harvard median standards
(Gomez scale), and mortality rates were followed up over two years. On
weight/height and height/age data, there was no link between death-rate
and MMU; but severely below-standard children showed three times the death
rates of all the others. On weight/age data, the 456 children tested as
normal (90%+ of Gomez scale) or mildly undernourished (75-90%) showed
somewhat lower mortality during the next two years than the moderately
undernourished (60-74%), at 36.6 and 42.1 per 1000 respectively - but
this pales into insignificance by contrast with the 112.4 per 1000 rate
suffered by the 427 children severely (i.e. over 60%) below weight/age
standards. 44/ Of the 34 children tested as severely undernourished at
1-2 years by height/age and weight/height standards, 8 were dead two years

afterwards   (<u>Nutrition Reviews</u>, <u>39</u>, 11, 1981, p.25).

The Narangwal (Punjab) study confirms that death-risk within a
year, among 5145 children aged 12-35 months, increased markedly only when
weight/age ratios fell below about 65% of the Harvard median, but among
children aged 1-11.9 months there appears to have been a sharp decrease
in death-rates, even between mild and zero undernourishment measured by
weight for age (i.e. at 80% of Harvard median)   (Kielmann and McCord,
1978, p. 1248). However, weight-for-age data reflect recent illness and
parasites, not just food intake - especially over a shortish follow-up
period.   Comparison of the Narangwal results with Chen's data show Chen's
height/age indicators clearly indicating that - while severe shortfalls
were associated with grossly increased subsequent risk of death - moderate
and mild ones were weakly associated even in a 0-11 month follow-up, but not
at all over a 0-23 month period (Sukhatme, 1982, Table 10).

The use of weight/age (rather than height/weight, height/age, or
growth curve) standards also embodies - apart from nutrition, infection
and parasites - high birth-order and low birth-weight as predictors of
death-risk, since both (although inversely intercorrelated) tend to reduce
weight-for-age and to raise infant and child mortality (Taylor <u>et al</u>.,
1981, pp. 15, 18; Newland, 1981, pp. 22, 39-40).

The literally vital importance of avoiding <u>severe</u> undernutrition
and its anthropometric effects on under-fives, and the near-unimportance
of MMU, have a physical basis. Shortage of food reduces resistance to
infection mainly by damaging immune response, and may worsen this process by
damaging intestinal absorption of the already-inadequate diet; but Sukhatme
concluded, from a review of the evidence, that such "functions which are
thought to be affected in malnutrition ... are not altered in children unless
their body weight for age is so low as to be below 60% of the Harvard median
standard" (Sukhatme, 1981, p. 25). Reddy confirms that in his Indian sample
"only children who have weights below 60% of the Harvard standard or 80% of
the IMCR, who constitute 10% of the child population, have altered immunocompetence"; Kielmann's recent work suggests no impairment of nonspecific
immune capacity above 70% of Gomez weight-for-age standards (Reddy <u>et al</u>., 1976,
p. 6; Kielmann and Curcio, 1981, pp. 3-26). Although Chandra mentions
"growing evidence ... that even mild or moderate deficits may alter the
immunologic response of some undernourished children", he stresses that the
"proportion of [children with such deficits] who show immunologic [impairment]
is relatively small", and that "the impairment in immunocompetence is less
marked" (Chandra, 1981, p. 228). His other analyses suggest a threshold
effect in a major channel through which undernutrition may affect immunocompetence (the balance among T-cells) (Chandra, 1980), a result fully
compatible with Chen's indictment of severe malnutrition, as opposed to MMU,
as a cause of child deaths.

Moreover, synergism between undernutrition and infection, at least
if anthropometric shortfall is mild or moderate, may well operate in ways
implying that a more cost-effective attack on death and disease can be mounted
by reducing infection, or by dealing with it wisely, than by increasing
dietary intake. Oral rehydration with sugar, salt, and clean water -
instead of diet reduction - in most types of diarrhoea, and inoculation against
major infections (Rohde, 1982; Grant, 1982), are often more cost-effective
ways to improve nutritional status (and to save life) than are incentives,
advice, or medical overview that encourage people to use higher incomes in
ways that push children with MMU to "normal" anthropometry. Such a push
could displace their own more acute health, environmental, and other non-food

needs, and/or the more acute caloric needs among the severely underfed.

If so, effects on disease, death, and even anthropometry will be disappointing. Thus, among 100 children from the lower socio-economic groups in Cali (Bolivia), "nutritional availability did not relate significantly to the growth measures [, and] effects of family income on weight and height of children were negligible, while effects of neighborhood factors" - plainly proxies for hygiene and exposure to infection as causes of growth faltering - "were strongly significant" (Nutrition Reviews, 1981, p. 329). Sukhatme blames earlier worm-loads and infections for most of the anthropometric lag of Indian 2-3 year-olds behind their US counterparts, adding: "No amount of food can correct diarrheal disease or even significantly decrease its incidence" (Sukhatme, 1981, pp. 24-5). As regards capacity to absorb food, severely damaged in kwashiorkor, "no gross defects ... have yet been described in children" with MMU - whereas "preliminary studies in Guatemala indicate that moderate diarrhea may result in an increased loss of calories in the stool of 500 to 600 calories per day" (Ebrahim, 1979, pp. 66-7).

(iv) Hence lighter people normally need fewer calories
    After age 29, extra weight means only more fat (p. 14). After age 13, caloric requirements are per kg., irrespective of age (p.14). Even for under-fives (unless severely undernourished), extra calories probably bring little or no improvement in death-rates, school performance, or adult physical productivity (pp. 15-19). Thus estimates of income or outlay needed to afford DERs should - normally and on present evidence - set them in LDCs almost in proportion to the lower weight of their populations, especially (pp. 14, 21, 24, 25 and fn. 57) the poorer sections. "Normally" means "except to allow for catch-up growth in severe child undernutrition, and for post-famine recovery". "On present evidence" means that some suspicions of possible damage from MMU remain. However, these count for much less than the high risk of grave damage from severe states. "First things first" - the normal principle of diminishing marginal utility - means that scarce resources to raise caloric intake, by reducing poverty or otherwise, should be concentrated, to begin with, on families with severely undernourished children.

Since low-income families in developing countries devote 60-85% of outlay to food, it is sensible to call them

    - "ultra-poor" whenever they cannot afford enough calories, per unit weight, to avoid substantial risk of severe undernutrition; but also

    - "moderately poor" whenever they can afford enough calories, per unit weight, to avoid ultra-poverty, but not substantial risk of MMU and its associated hunger, non-food deprivation, and possible residual medical hazard. 45/

Four papers confirm the probably adequate health and performance, in warm-to-hot LDCs, of children with MMU. E. Downs (1964) found that 131 Lebanese children aged 1-3, followed up for 12 months, showed height/age and weight/age, but not weight/height (Seckler, 1980, pp. 1-3, 7-11), in the moderately undernourished range. Yet "clinically [they] presented a favorable picture. The majority were well-proportioned and alert, and over 70% were rated "good-excellent on overall impressions of responsiveness, vigor, muscle tone, skin turgor and color". Downs adds: "Their accomplishments, however, seemed more commensurate with their [retarded height and weight] than with their age" (E. Downs, 1964, p.80), but commented, "My impression is that all this would be caught up in normal maturing" (E. Downs, personal communication, August 14, 1981).

Second, and especially significant in view of Downs's results, Seckler has shown that 80-90% of children classified as anthropometrically undernourished were "usually short for their age, but had the proper weight for their short height" and that Indian evidence suggests that such children become healthy adults. Indeed height/age and weight/age shortfalls appear to do little harm provided that weight/height is adequate (Seckler, 1980, pp. 2, 8-11), at least after the age of five or so. Is a value-judgement needed? 46/

Third, Tanner's work links even weight/height shortfalls, if moderate, to a long-run selection effect of climate, corresponding to the medium-run effects discussed on pp. 12-14. He writes: "There is, in fact, a quite close correlation between ... weight per unit height [in] adults, and the average annual temperature" (Tanner, 1978, p. 139) - among groups with MMU.

Fourth, work in New Guinea showed hardly any clinical signs of undernutrition among children aged 1-18 with substantial dietary energy (calorie) shortfalls. "Current standards may be set too high for some groups [, or] adaptations ... occur that are not disclosed by the usual techniques of assessing nutritional status". Since available food was not eaten although "bulk did not restrict intake", it is concluded that probably calorie/age ratios for low weight-for-age populations - even among young children - overestimate requirements, so that cals/kg. better indicate the adequacy of dietary energy intakes (Ferro-Luzzi et al., 1975, pp. 1443, 1451). This is especially important in view of the many New Guinean studies used as a basis for claims of widespread undernutrition.

3. Infections and parasites

These are certainly much more prevalent in LDCs (Ebrahim, 1979, p.62). Severe, but probably not other, child undernutrition significantly cuts resistance to infection (pp. 17-19). This helps to justify "ultra-poverty lines" where outlay (or income) increases would not much decrease severe undernutrition, and with it infection.

Do the diverse nutritional costs of fighting these more frequent infections (Ebrahim, 1979, p. 64-6) and of sharing food with parasites such as roundworm, substantially increase DERs - and outlay needed to afford them - in LDC environments? This might seem obvious, but is probably not the case, owing to three facts and two points of logic.

The first fact is that many ill people reduce work or play activity and thereby cut their DERs - to an unknown extent among poor people in LDCs; this could largely offset any increase in DERs to fight the illness. Second, undernutrition during infection is often due to food habits, especially to reduced ingestion during infant diarrhoea; extra income will scarcely affect adequacy of diets in infection under these circumstances. Third, the synergism between infection and undernutrition - normally likely to be important only when the latter is severe - is particularly threatening at the age of 7 to 15 months, during weaning (Kielmann et al., 1978, p. 37). Principal problems here are the bulk of many weaning foods (Korte, 1974, p.3; Chaudhuri, 1982, at fn. 33) and the uncleanness of water. Low-income families will be most severely exposed, but unless undernutrition is severe, they are once again likeliest to be helped by more access to publicly financed medical care than by simply "more food".

As for the logic, the first point relates to age-structure. In LDCs the main sufferers from infection are small children. Even if infection raises net caloric needs by 40%, the absolute extra requirement is much smaller than in adults. Second, on the logic of policy: even if mild-to-moderate undernutrition and environmental exposure to infection interact as causes of child deaths, environment often plays the leading part (see the Cali case on p. 19). Extra social outlay to reduce environmental parasites, bacteria and vectors - while often complex and costly - can be more cost-effective in combating illness and mortality than extra private income to buy more food, itself shared with uninfected family members, bacteria, and parasites. Personal nutrition (and private income) could matter more than public health (and social spending) only where undernutrition is severe, but we do not know enough to be sure. ·

4. Pregnancy and lactation

Women of childbearing age spend a larger proportion of time pregnant or lactating in LDCs than in DCs. This is mainly because family size norms are higher; an average couple needs more pregnancies to obtain the same likelihood of a given number of live births, more live births to obtain the same likelihood of a given number of healthy adult descendants, and more descendants to obtain the same likelihood that one of them will support the couple in its old age. This latter requirement is far more acute in LDCs, which seldom have social security, and greatly influences LDC family size norms. Lactation requirements are also greater, because children typically stay longer at the breast than in developed countries; this probably does somewhat reduce extra pregnancy DERs (by prolonging post-partum amennorhoea), but DERs for both pregnancies and lactations are further increased, even above the high family size norms, by ignorance of birth control. All these factors operate more strongly in the poorest families, already at greatest risk of undernutrition.

However, we cannot infer that the requirements of pregnancy and lactation increase per kg. DERs in LDCs (relative to DCs), especially for moderately poor families, whose low income-per-CU involves risks of MMU "only". Suppose we define a population's pregnancy and lactation multiplier (PLM) as its total kcal-DER on an average day, divided by that DER minus the number of kcals required to fuel pregnancy and lactation. Such a PLM need not be higher for LDCs, or for their moderately poor people than for their non-poor. There are three reasons why not.

First, although the average (and even more the poor) woman of childbearing age in an LDC is likelier to be pregnant or lactating than her DC counterpart, the average person in an LDC is much less likely to be a woman of childbearing age. A much larger proportion of persons is below that age, because so many die before reaching it; because median age of menarche is higher (p. 22, fn. 48); and because the fertile period ends earlier. All three facts, in LDCs, apply especially to poor families. Therefore, the average (and especially the poor) person in an LDC may well be less, not more, likely than in a DC to need extra calories because of pregnancy or lactation. This cuts back the PLM in poor countries.

Second, extra DERs per day pregnant or lactating in LDCs are them-selves reduced by the relatively low weights and heights of women and sucklings (especially in poor households) - except to the extent that such low sizes are damaging and the result of inadequate caloric intake. In

MMU (or in multi-generational poverty of the "small but healthy") the low sizes are probably often adaptive, harmless, not to be usefully altered by changed caloric intake, and/or due to interpersonal variations in food-to-work conversion efficiency (pp.25-34). Weights or heights low in this way, among mothers or infants, do justify lower PLMs in poor countries and families - even though, in 1-2 generations, more food brings sizes nearer to DC levels (fn. 46).

Third, larger proportions of women of childbearing age participate in strenuous work in LDCs, especially in poor families, than in DCs. To the extent that they reduce such work in late pregnancy or early lactation, their net PLM is reduced, as compared with women similarly reducing less strenuous work. (However, pushing the PLM in the opposite direction is the fact that, at a given strenuousness of work, poorer women usually want to continue working closer to childbirth, and to resume working sooner afterwards, than better-off women; but this wish is made hard to fulfill by the lesser access of very poor families 47/ to extended or three-generation family support.)

Apart from this, five considerations make it dubious whether - in MMU - more private income, to be used to provide more calories in pregnancy and lactation, will cost-effectively improve health, even if the PLM is indeed high. First, some of the caloric shortfall among pregnant women (as among infected children) is due to food habits, not low income; the evidence from Calcutta does not suggest that extra couple income, even if earned by pregnant and lactating women, efficiently handles that problem (Reutlinger and Selowsky, 1976). Second, (again like infection), uncompleted, otherwise "non-adult-generating", or simply unwanted pregnancies may be "better" prevented by contraception (as infection may be better prevented by sanitation), rather than accommodated by maternal calories. Third, LDCs' longer lactation means lower external DERs for children - not just more for mothers; the former should be set against possibly higher PLMs. Fourth, in many LDCs, uncompleted and unwanted pregnancies, and family size norms, are indeed falling, with improved education (especially female), health, and general development; as this happens, any remaining excess of PLMs in poor countries, and in moderately poor families within them, will shrink further.

Fifth, this decline of PLMs with development could be retarded by any process, other than rising income, to induce normal or mildly undernourished women to eat more in order to meet over-high requirements of pregnancy and lactation. Nutritional levels in lactation, even if below apparent requirements, appear to be associated with "adaptive changes ... so the energy balance is maintained"; a recent Gambian study, in which 1000 kcal/day were added for 12 months during pregnancy and early lactation, showed "no marked improvement in body weight", but rises in plasma prolactin levels, possibly heralding a faster return of fertility after the birth, to "undo all the benefits of food supplementation". Apart from this specific effect on fertility, higher caloric intake at a given level of physical activity (or lower activity at a given intake) is associated with earlier menarche, shorter birth intervals, and later menopause. 48/ Non-income-related measures to achieve such higher intake, e.g. food supplementation or nutritional advice - including the powerful weapon of setting "poverty lines" based on over-high recommended intakes - could even, if implemented before general development has reduced family size norms or increased access to contraception, be counter-productive for the normal or mildly-undernourished mother. She is unlikely, by eating more, to save, or improve the quality of, her or her children's lives; she is likelier to increase the probable number of children born, thus reducing their life-chances (especially their probable school performance) and probably, by cruel irony, their chances to avoid undernourishment later.

The evidence from such food supplementation programs, moreover, casts further doubt on "more income - more food in pregnancy - higher birth-weight" as an efficient sequence for saving infant lives in face of maternal MMU. INCAP's Guatemalan experiment 49/ showing clear gains to particular children from (once-for-all and carefully supervised) food supplementation to their mothers during pregnancy, does not dispose of the possibility that total child populations could fail to gain, or even could lose, if maternal fertility rises as suggested above. Moreover, this unique (but costly) 1972 pilot has apparently nowhere "been applied in a field setting" (Rohde, 1982a); a review of 200 supervised child feeding programs in such real-life conditions found (a) non-participation rates of 20-75% even with mostly free food, (b) use by unintended beneficiaries of 30-35% of the food supplement. 50/ Extra family income, in the hope of generating extra food for pregnant mothers, is even more vulnerable than supervised child feeding to such diversion.

These arguments seem decisive only against upgrading PLMs for the moderately poor (and for LDCs as a whole). For the very poor - those at risk of severe undernourishment - the extra needs of an already emaciated mother (and of a deprived fetus and infant), alongside the proven harm to health, and to mental and physical performance, of prolonged severe under-nourishment argue clearly for an increased PLM. Pregnancy and lactation, like other factors in this chapter, justify both an "extreme poverty" definitional borderline more rigorously than the "moderate poverty" borderline associated with risk of MMU, and concentration of both income and nutrition policies upon the 10-20% of LDC populations in extreme poverty.

5. Age-structure

FAO/WHO and national DERs are specific to age-groups. In a rough-and-ready way, therefore, the fact that populations in poor countries contain a much larger proportion of infants (0-1) and small children (1-5) (UN, 1980) - so that they need fewer calories than a population of similar size, but typically with a much larger proportion of adults, in DCs - is taken account of in DERs. For example, FAO/WHO's DERs for infants are more than doubled by age 4, and further raised (by 74% for males, 42% for females) between age 4 and and adulthood (FAO/WHO, 1973, p. 34); this duly lowers the typical LDC ratio of requirements-per-person to requirements-per-consumer-unit, as compared to typical DC ratios.

In three ways, however, requirements in LDCs' at-risk groups tend to be overstated by inadequate allowance for their relatively young age, as compared to DCs. First, people's DERs are assessed by the age-group into which they fall; but higher death-rates in LDCs mean that, especially among under-fives, the proportion at the "young end" of each age-group is considerably larger than in a comparable DC. Hence the effect of applying a "DC average" requirement to an LDC age-group - at least during the first 10-15 years of life, while that requirement is rising rapidly with age - is to overstate the within-group average age, and hence average requirement, of the LDC. For example, of 100 new-born children in Bangladesh or Bolivia, about 85 will be alive by age 1, as against 98 in industrialised countries (World Tables, 1980). The average age of non-survivors at death, in both cases, is at most three months. Since average requirements in the first three months are at most 500 kcal/day, but over the whole first year about 820 kcals/day (Ebrahim, 1979, p. 39; FAO/WHO, 1973, pp. 33-5), the use of a DC average DER for "age-group 0-1" would - because of that group's younger average age in LDCs - overstate that group's typical LDC require-ments by at least 5.4%. 51/

Second, the whole age-structure is especially weighted towards infants and small children - with consequent falls in the DER <u>per person</u> - in poor households (Srinivasan, 1981, p. 12), a point frequently neglected in estimates of DERs and hence of poverty lines (ILO/JASPA, 1980, Appendix G (2), p. 39; Lipton, WBSWP, 1983) If - as is often the case - the DERs of households of a given size are estimated from national, instead of income-group-specific, information about households age-structure, then the relative requirements of poor, at-risk households will be overestimated. 52/

Third, the above two effects interact. Not only (for poor households) are the proportions of persons in age-groups requiring fewer calories (infants and small children) in many cases first underestimated by using national average structures of age-groups, and then again underestimated by using developed-country assumptions for age-structures <u>within</u> those groups; these underestimates are multiplicative.

Two qualifications are needed. First - as always - these downward adjustments of a few percentage-points in requirements,while they may mean safety for the moderately poor, are unlikely to prevent the ultra-poor from risking severe undernourishment. Second, the process of development itself eliminates these three factors: as people, especially poor people, in LDCs acquire command over more income, so their age-structures (among and within age-groups) approach those of DCs. This very process of development, however, is likely to involve acquisition of more calories. While under-development causes high infant and child death-rates, it also creates age-structures that reduce DERs in the families especially vulnerable to those high rates; the process by which death-rates fall, apart from changing age-structures in ways that increase per-person DERs, also normally involves increased command over calories.

6. Work

It is often suggested that generally harder physical work raises caloric needs, and hence the "poverty line" outlay needed to afford them, in LDCs and especially among the poorest there. Longhurst's Nigerian data suggest that poor people are often in an "energy trap", requiring them (especially at the margin) to expend many more calories per 100 calories' worth of purchasing-power than the non-poor (Longhurst, 1981). Comparison between agricultural labor and sedentary work, awareness of search costs (usually requiring walking), and measurement and observation of the duration and caloric requirements of many domestic tasks, notably water-carrying (Schofield, 1978, passim; Fox, 1953; Batliwala, 1982, esp. Tables 2 & 5), strongly suggest that work in LDCs increases DERs more than elsewhere - especially for the poor, who are likeliest to use up many calories in working.

Clearly, work "per-kilogram-hour" of body-weight is generally more demanding in LDCs, and particularly for at-risk groups. However, we cannot infer that DERs of work "per-person-year" are therefore greater, either absolutely or as a proportion of BMR, for nutritionally vulnerable inhabitants of poor countries than for Westerners. Suppose that (as with pregnancy and lactation, p.21) we construct a "work multiplier" or WM: the ratio of total DERs, on an average day, to what those DERs would be with no requirements for work to earn one's living. Would the WM necessarily be greater in a rich country - or household - than in a poor one?

In an LDC, especially for the poor:
- The intensity of a typical hour of work, per kg. of bodyweight per working person, is certainly greater, pushing the WM up; however, four other factors cut the WM:
- The proportion of persons of working age is smaller (see pp. 23-24);
- Participation among these, especially for the poorest, may be cut, e.g. by illness; 53/
- During prolonged slack seasons, productive agricultural effort often pays for only a couple of hours a day, often in artificially extended cattle-care or domestic work that shrinks dramatically in the peak season; 54/
- Muscle weight, and hence "available" effective caloric effort, per worker, is smaller;
- Fat weight, and hence energy wasted while walking and working, is smaller.

* * *

My hunch is that the WM (due to a lower "DER for productive and domestic work" per person per year) is less in LDCs, especially among the poor, than in DCs, even though the typical worker has to put out more calories per hour per kg. of body-weight, especially if poor. This hunch needs testing against local data sets.

However, the conclusion of this section is clear. Climate, weight and age-structure substantially reduce DERs per CU in LDCs as compared with DCs, and for the poor in LDCs especially. The reduction is considerably more - and supposed offsetting factors (work intensity, infections, pregnancy and lactation) "offset", if at all, much less than standard comparisons indicate.

(f) Inter- and intrapersonal variations further cut requirements

These are the most controversial factors claimed to reduce DERs among the apparently (but not severely) undernourished. "Interpersonal variation" is the alleged tendency for persons with below-average lifetime caloric intakes per kg. also to have below-average requirements. "Intrapersonal variation" is the alleged capacity of the body, faced over limited periods with limited amounts of shortfall of intake behind ASAG average DER per kg. of body-weight, to adapt by increasing the efficiency with which it converts intake into energy.55/ Given the controversy - and without concealing that I am convinced by Dr. Sukhatme's arguments (Sukhatme, 1977, 1981, 1982; Srinivasan, 1981; Dandekar, 1981, 1982) - I should emphasize that the main case for separate benchmarks for ultra-poverty (involving risk from undernutrition) and moderate poverty lies in the arguments of pp. 9-25, without any considerations of variability in DERs per kg. of body-weight. Past FAO/WHO requirements 56/ have been set well above true Western average DERs per kg.; and the "translation" of these into LDC averages, especially for poor households, has not involved enough reduction.

The latter fact, indeed, arises largely because "translators" have often ignored one sort of variability. The younger age-structures and lower adult body-weights of poorer LDC households are seldom allowed for, and per-person requirements are calculated at local or national average body-weights (and even sometimes age-structures). 57/ However, variability in DERs per person, due to age and to adult body-weight, tends to cause poorer LDC households to need less food, to avoid risky undernutrition, than such calculations suggest.

Variability probably reduces DERs per kg. of body-weight as well.

However, this argument is not needed to make the case that only an ultra-poor subset of persons below the poverty line is at risk of undernourishment. Indeed, variability in DERs per kg. genuinely strengthens that case only to the extent that "double counting" - e.g. deducting "for variability" below a DER, like that of the 1977 World Food Survey, already reduced to allow for it - is avoided.58/ However, variability per kg. is so important - in constructing poverty lines, in defining the nutritional characteristics of the poor, and in devising nutritional and other policies against poverty - that the issue cannot be avoided here.

* * *

FAO/WHO stress that their recommended DER per kg., in any ASAG, is an average for person-days in that group (FAO/WHO, p. 10; FAO, 1974, p. 2). Persons eating below (above) that average per kg. on any particular day, or even for many days, are therefore not necessarily under- (over-)nourished. Similarly, the per-kg. gap between an individual's intake on one day (or even many successive days) and his average ASAG requirement need not measure his under- or over-nourishment. With some modification,59/ these remarks also hold for per-kg. gaps between individual intakes and the lower average DERs suggested on pp.9-25.

Thus no single income or outlay per person is definitely "just enough" - given ASAG, prices and spending patterns and even given also body-weight - to meet requirements, i.e. to decide if that person is under-nourished (because of poverty or otherwise). If the total effect of interpersonal and intrapersonal variation in requirements within an ASAG is large,60/ the divergence of person-day requirements from group averages could cause many people to be wrongly classified as undernourished-because-poor, when in fact they earn and/or spend enough to meet their (below-ASAG-average) per kg. requirements - Type I error. Conversely, many people could be classified as not undernourished-because-poor when, because of unusually high DERs per kg., they in fact are so - Type II error.

This could cause serious classificatory, and therefore policy, errors if Type I errors are concentrated on some seasons, places, or ASAGs, and Type II errors on others. We do not know if this is the case (although substantial variations across Indian State samples in intakes per CU, unmatched by corresponding variations in ASAG structure or in clinical undernutrition, suggest that it is). That is because too little is yet known about cause or effect of interpersonal or intra-personal variation in requirements per kg., and especially in their adaptability to low intakes (above all among under-fives), with or without harmful side-effects, for periods of different lengths and for shortfalls of different proportions. Lack of such knowledge is perhaps the most serious gap in our understanding of "characteristics of poor and poorest groups". Such knowledge might drastically change our assessment of the characteristics of people too poor to eat enough - of the subsets, e.g. regions, of population where ultra-poverty was most prevalent.

However, in a total, large, diverse national population, would variations in DERs per kg. alter our estimate of proportions too poor to eat enough? Common sense suggests not; would not the numbers of Type I and of Type II errors be about the same? Suppose that, for the average person (or person-day) in each ASAG, average DER and intake are correctly estimated; but that we know nothing about the two distributions except that in each ASAG (a) each is symmetric about the mean, (b) the two are statistically independent.61/ Then, for each person (or person-day) "below ASAG average intake but not undernourished because as far, or further, below average DER", the best expectation is 1.0 other persons (or person-days) "above ASAG average intake but undernourished, because as far, or further, above average requirements".

However, such common sense fails us, because both assumptions - symmetry and independence - are false, in ways that reduce the incidence of undernourishment in total populations, as compared with what it would be if all ASAG members (whatever their intakes) required ASAG average daily calories per kg. of body-weight. (In other words, Type I errors far exceed Type II errors). The reductions happen both directly and via effects through income; and they operate through the DER distribution both among persons over their lifetimes, and among the days of each person's life.

* * *

Let us first assume no adjustments, e.g. correlation with past instances, in a person's DER per kg. We thus first consider the likely distribution only of lifetime intakes and requirements for a standardized set of lifetimes, each passing through similar ASAGs; say for males surviving to age 70, and enjoying, in each year of life, a given activity level. Such a standard male's per kg. daily (average lifetime) energy requirement (ALDR) increases with (a) his average BMR, and (b) the reciprocal of his efficiency in converting food to above-basal work. Item (b) may be substantially raised by (a) numerous, or large, "standard" (i.e. non-brown) fat cells, (b) the extent to which "brown fat" concentrations (associated with energetically wasteful metabolic processes) are retained to adulthood, (c) the frequency, composition, and exercise-related timing of given caloric intake (Miller, 1983, p. 197). 62/

Also, partly for the same reasons, BMR is variable, in part genetically, in part with activity patterns.63/ Even if variations in daily energy balance are almost all intra-individual (Sukhatme, 1982, p. 30; Widdowson,1947; Scrimshaw, 1972; Edholm, 1970) scope remains for "standard males" to show varying ALDR. First, this is because varying levels and fluc-tuations of intake and activity, among individuals, could lead to varying per-kg. efficiency in converting food to work. Second, fat/lean ratios (given body-weight) affect efficiency in converting physical work into tasks performed; fat people must use larger proportions of given energy output for unproductive work (hauling around their own fat) and must therefore work harder (and eat more) to secure a given income than others, of the same weight but less fat, in the same ASAG. Third, similarly, people with much brown fat may need to support less efficient metabolic processes than others. In any event, the populations found to have little inter-individual variation are homogeneous (and very small).

Suppose ALDR (per kg.) for a population of these standard males is 30.5 kcals, and that their daily average intake is 28.5. Each male in this group would be - if all its members were at these averages! - 7% energy-undernourished on the average day of his life. However, it is more reasonable to hypothesize distributions rather like:

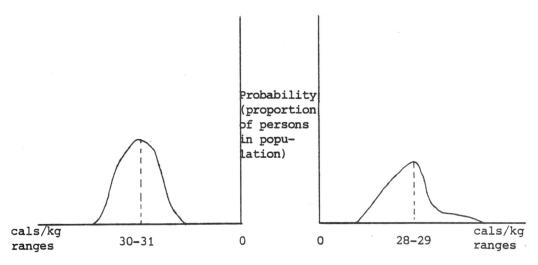

Daily requirements (life average)   Daily intake (life average)

Numbers of persons with cal/kg. observed to left and right of
the mode are the same in both diagrams. Being above average lifetime
daily intake (28.5 cals per kg.) could be about equiprobable with being
below it; so, most likely, is being above or below average ALDR (30.5 cals).
Yet numbers undernourished are reduced, and seriousness for these is
increased, by the breakdown of the symmetry assumption for intakes -
observed fact, not hypothesis, and perhaps biologically inevitable.64/
In the population intakes diagram, the long "tail" of above-average eaters,
none remotely likely to be undernourished, ensures more people with intake
above 28-29 (personal average requirement minus 7%) than below it (Beaton,
Annex to Reutlinger and Alderman, p.24); in the requirements diagram, one
would expect symmetry.

The breakdown of the independence assumption, between the two
diagrammed distributions, probably also reduces the numbers likely to be
undernourished.65/ Persons below mean intake per kg. are so for two
reasons: incapacity to achieve it, or deliberate choice not to do so. The
latter is likely to be associated, in part through the "appestat",66/ with
a position below the requirements mean also; similarly above the mean.
Among 54 East Javanese men of similar heights and weights, "output of
work [was] not affected by calorie intake ... average work output [on
six days, spread evenly over the year, as a proportion of] average
energy intake ... was 80% higher for ten subjects with lowest energy
intake, compared to ten with the highest". Another week-long study 67/
among this group showed that the 5 men with highest intake showed BMRs
"almost twice" those of the 5 lowest.68/ Among people who have kcal
intakes per day (averaged across their lifetimes) below the average DERs
for their ASAGs, many are thus because their bodies are relatively
efficient - featuring BMRs below ASAG averages, and/or efficiencies in
converting food to above-basal work, for most of these people's lifetimes.
Such bodies "signal" lower DER than their ASAG average. These bodies are
not undernourished. If their intakes are raised, they metabolise faster,
or accumulated largely useless body fat (or extra pregnancies: p. 22 and
fn. 48). Among the poor, these are the people who - though ingesting
below ASAG average (albeit not their own) lifetime DERs - sensibly choose
not to spend extra income on food (Shah, 1979).

This largely accounts for the major divergences, even over long
periods, 69/ in calorie intakes per kg. among persons in the same income-
group and ASAG. In low-income groups, that divergence indicates either

that people who are below average DER deliberately eat less than others, or (implausibly) that such people tolerate gross and prolonged under-nourishment, when they could, as others at their income-level do, act otherwise.

Interactions through income strengthen the "dependence" of the two diagrammed distributions. Income inequality - while undesirably broadening out the intake-distribution diagram - also ensures that poor people are likelier to be found to be left of the mean both on that diagram and on the requirement diagram, while richer people are likelier to be to the right of both means. Through several mechanisms, income inequality - while helping to create both poverty-induced hunger and affluent obesity - acts, both on its own and jointly with the appestat, to limit those evils. Inherited effects reinforce the "positive" statistical interdependence of the two diagrammed distributions of calories/kg. Other effects probably reduce poor people's relative requirement of calories per person.

First, the hereditary mechanism. In many societies, most poor people - those having to spend 70-80% or more of outlay on food - have parents, grandparents, etc. who were similarly poor. The more such "generations of poverty" there have been in a family, the likelier it is that most family members are "genetically" well to the left of the requirements mean; for infants and children, unable to use calories efficiently enough to thrive at levels of kcals/day below the averages for their ASAGs, would - if too poor to meet those requirements - be unlikely to reach childbearing age. Part of such "ability to thrive at low intakes" is related to low height and weight, but if this goes too far it reduces later capacity to get work and earn income to support families; much of the inherited "ability to thrive at low intakes" in children (as of later capacity, especially in lean years or seasons, to get work as adults) is therefore, in "hereditarily poor" families, related to efficiency in the sense of low caloric requirement per kg., given the work output (i.e. either low BMR or high conversion efficiency of food into above-basal work). Experimental work in the USA suggests that reduced calorie intake at given activity levels cuts BMR by over 40% in some subjects, but by much less in others (New York Times, May 19, 1982); of course, poor people do not have a distinct gene pool (see fn. 46), but per-haps those born with genes of the "BMR responsive" type 70/ can best tolerate low caloric intakes, and hence survive poverty, over several generations.

This is the main way in which "hereditarily low income" is likely to select persons with below-average caloric requirements, 71/ensuring "positive interdependence" between the two diagrams (so that many fewer people are "too poor to eat enough" than have "low income and lifetime daily caloric intake below ALDR per kg. for their ASAGs"). The second way concerns mobilizable body reserves - the fat/lean ratio. Here what is desirable, for survival through poverty, differs between two distinct environments.

If fluctuations in nutritional stress are relatively few, short and mild for the poorest 20-40%, whereas their average shortfall behind requirements of daily and yearly command over food, from cash income plus own-farm food-growing, is relatively large (as compared in each case with places at similar income-levels), then poor people's survival prospects - and their chances to produce children who themselves survive into procreative age-groups - are increased by genes favoring deposition of very

low proportions, say 4-8% in men, of body-weight as fat. This makes
tropical work easier and more effective: first, because muscle-power
is greater, relative to fat body-weight (needing to be pushed and
pulled uselessly around to, from and at work, while burning up dietary
energy); and second, because lean people's sweating-area is greater
relative to body-volume (Lee, 1957). In several other tropical
environments, however, fluctuations in nutritional stress over time
(long slack seasons, droughts, infections or work peaks sharply raising
nutritional requirements) are, for the poor, more serious - commoner,
longer or more severe (and/or harder to provide against) - as compared
to the average level of shortfall. Here, genes favoring the deposition
of a somewhat higher proportion of body-weight - say 10-15% in men - as
fat, especially in forms (fn. 62) that are economic and readily
mobilized in hard times, would probably maximize poor people's prospects
of multi-generation survival and family-formation.

In both sorts of environment, the pressures on generations of
"hereditarily poor" probably select those with locally optimal fat/lean
ratios at given calorie intakes per kg. But efficiency in using calories
involves different things in different places for the tropical poor. Where
unexpected fluctuation is the main enemy, less-lean people gain (apart from
the medium-term effect above) in the short term because they "conserve
more of their ingested carbohydrate as liver glycogen for use between
meals, and thereby avoid the high energy cost of fat synthesis" (Naismith
et al., 1982, p. 19) - though even there the poor cannot afford to support very
high fat/lean ratios. Where low (though steady) requirement-intake ratios
are poor people's main problem, survival chances may well be optimized
by genes that tend to cut back the fat proportion of body-weight, so
the body's bulk contains less "waste" to service with food. In either
case, families "poor for generations" are likelier to survive, despite
poverty, if their genes lead them to the fat/lean ratios making the locally
best use of scarce dietary calories. Hence such families' DERs, as well
as intakes, per kg. of body-weight are pushed down by poverty.

These inherited effects of poverty on ALDRs - in places where
infant mortality averages 100-200 yearly - can operate in two or three
generations (though genuine "evolution" takes hundreds). So it is
probable that families, long forced by poverty into low intakes, have
"selected" (for survival and procreation) those with genetically low
requirements - high conversion efficiencies, low BMRs, appropriate
fat/lean ratios.

Non-inherited effects of poverty on food required per person are
less clear, but probably on balance reinforce the effects of inheritance.
It has been argued that - although the poor may be pushed to the left of
mean population DERs by low adult weight, high child/adult ratios, and
high unemployment - they are pushed rightwards by their more physically
demanding employment and household chores, by greater proneness to pregnancy
and infection, and by a lower ratio of old people to prime adults (Reutlinger
and Alderman, 1980, p. 8). More empirical work is needed, but, among these non-
inherited factors, those associating moderate poverty with reduced requirements are likely to prevail over countervailing factors by a big margin
(pp. 12-25). Most of the latter factors are "defused" by poor people's
lower weight and higher child/adult ratios. For example, among the poor,
high child/adult ratios reduce the proportion of persons requiring support
in the event of heavy exertion or pregnancy, and low adult body-weights
reduce the "kgs. per person" requiring such support. In MMU, these

parallel reductions in intake and requirements - though associated with poverty and with boring, unsatisfying diets - have no obvious ill-effects on health.

Another non-hereditary income process may help to correlate below-average (ASAG) lifetime intakes with below-average ALDRs. A major motive for long, hard effort is to obtain food. This applies especially where, as among the poor, large parts of income are spent on food. Presumably above-average ALDRs intensify (and below-average ALDRs moderate) the incentive to work, access to income, and therefore food intake.

*   *   *

The above evidence, that below-average dietary energy intakes (especially if associated with poverty) greatly increase the probability that the victims have relatively low requirements, relates to ALDRs for sets of "lifetimes" passing through a given series of activity-groups. A person's "lifetime average requirement" may differ from another person's in the same ASAG, even if their weights 72/ as well as lifespans are identical, for three reasons: interpersonal variations in BMR or in above-BMR food-to-work conversion efficiency; distinct patterns of intrapersonal variations, about the same lifetime moving averages, in energy intake or expenditure; and interpersonal variations in adjustment to intrapersonal variations (IVAIV). The above (pp.25-30) arguments were applied to inter-personal variations, but most of them carry over to distinct patterns of intrapersonal variations, and some to IVAIV. We next deal with the controversial issue of "intrapersonal variation" among the poor; then discuss IVAIV, which is probably of more policy significance but which is almost unresearched; and conclude by asking how the debate affects our views of the numbers, location, timing, and characteristics of "the poor and the poorest".

Random intrapersonal variation in requirements, symmetric about the mean, and uncorrelated with random and symmetric intrapersonal variation in intake, would (just as with interpersonal variation) not alter the extent, severity, or types of person-days affected by poverty-induced undernutrition. A particular day, on which I wake up with above or below average requirements, might or might not be a day when my intake is above or below normal. Intrapersonal variation affects the incidence of undernutrition - poverty-induced or other - only if there exist mechanisms adjusting intake and requirements, benignly (in the same direction) or perversely (which would increase the incidence of undernutrition).

Sukhatme's analysis strongly suggests some benign adjustment. There is a bounded auto-regressive stochastic process: between limits, the expected value of today's calorie requirements per kg. (given age, sex and work) increases with the value of today's, and to a lesser extent yesterday's, the day before yesterday's, etc., intakes. Sukhatme stresses the choice of metabolic pathways (Sukhatme, 1978) - routes by which food is mobilized for work - as the way in which a body, undernourished yester-day, shifts the probability-distribution of its requirements leftwards today; to his mechanisms there may be added possible reductions in the proportion of work that is bioenergetically "paid for" by the costly process of (brown-fat-mediated) non-diet induced thermogenesis. 73/ In the switch of pathways on which Sukhatme mainly relies, short-term conversion efficiency is increased by using food energy directly as glucose instead of converting to fat and then releasing it (ibid., p. 1383); however,

medium-term conversion of spare dietary energy to fat, not lean, is more
efficient if intake-mean requirement ratios vary seasonally (Payne and
Dugdale, 1977). Adjustment via pathway-switching must therefore, if it
exists, be very complex. Nor is it the only way in which Sukhatme can
be right. He cites evidence from Margen and Edmundson that low intake
could slow down the "body clock" by cutting BMR (Sukhatme, 1978; see
above, p. 29); or the efficiency of particular pathways can be varied,
in ways analogous to "training effect". 74/

What these possibilities have in common is the capacity of the
body to adjust its "efficiency", within limits, to earlier shortfalls.
The evidence for that capacity - from careful work showing that weight
and work change very little even during quite substantial and prolonged
changes in food intake - is indeed considerable, 75/ though major areas
of ignorance persist. 76/ The key questions for policy against poverty-
related undernutrition. are: what are the limits? And: do bodies differ
in the extent of adjustment capacity (and can they be helped to do
better)?

Homeostatic models of adjustment have, in addition to "good"
self-correcting features within those limits, "bad" features of cumulative
disorder outside them. 77/ These bad features loom especially large in
stochastic systems, because these show growing risks of malfunction as
the borderlines of normally effective homeostasis are approached; in
other words, the limits themselves are fuzzy, and even an approach risks
catastrophe. 78/ We need to know, about daily shortfalls in intake below
a body's long-run normal requirement per kg.:

 - how much can be tolerated - by bodies in different circumstances
(e.g. physically hard-worked, lactating, infant) - for 1, 2, 3, ...
consecutive days, with a probability below .01, .05 ... that homeostatic
limits in upward adjustment of bodily efficiency (and hence in downward
adjustment of requirements) will be exceeded with seriously damaging
results?

 - how long can these various "bodies" tolerate varying sizes of
shortfall (i.e. calories per kg. per day), with probability below .01,
.05, ... of damagingly exceeding homeostatic limits?

The answers should affect resource allocation against undernutrition,
and especially policies to prevent or anticipate risks of bad seasons or
years. The answers tell us who is ultra-poor, poor or non-poor. 79/
Short-cut attempts to "count the poor", by assuming a reduced requirements
level that supposedly "allows for homeostasis" because it cuts back the
estimated numbers undernourished to accord with clinical observations, 80/
do not satisfactorily avoid the problems raised by the need to define
those limits.

The other gap in our knowledge relates to chosen behavioral,
rather than to involuntary bodily, homeostasis. Suppose a body can, when
daily intake falls 10%, maintain work levels and cut requirements via
higher conversion efficiency. To what extent will different groups of
people choose not to reduce work (above BMR), so that their bodies in
fact raise conversion efficiency? Falling food availability probably
signifies a lower "price" for effort in terms of food-wage. If
substitution-effect outweighs income-effect, the body's owner will
replace income (and work) by leisure; the body, and the economy, then
achieve homeostasis in response to food intake below average requirement,
not mainly by increased food-work conversion efficiency, but mainly by
lower levels of effort, income and especially savings and growth.

Therefore, if (as seems very likely) requirements do adjust to intakes in a bounded stochastic autoregressive process, we need to know, not only its scope and limits, but also when and where people will choose to let it operate (i.e. to respond to lower intake, not by reduced work, but by increased efficiency) - and how that choice can be made less risky and costly for them, and more rewarding in terms of rapidly restored, pleasanter (if less conversion-efficient) and higher ratios of caloric intakes to requirement.

We are especially ignorant about how infants and small children respond (because the few generally quoted studies of homeostasis are for adults). 81/ What is the probability-distribution of the reductions they can tolerate via increased conversion efficiency or reduced BMR, and for how long? Will they choose to rely on such homeostasis when caloric intakes fall, i.e. to maintain work (i.e. play) - and, if not, with what side-effects on emotional or intellectual maturing?

A central problem is: how do groups (occupational, locational, genetic, etc.) differ in the periods and/or intensity of their capacity for homeostasis, and in the income-leisure indifference maps that might lead them to choose or reject such homeostasis, as opposed to adjustment of activity levels, when the food-value of returns to labor changes? We have seen (p.22 and fn. 48) that some groups of pregnant and lactating women appear to be unusually well equipped to tolerate under-nutrition without harm to mother or child. Presumably such IVAIV problems apply to most ASAGs whole age and sex spectrum: how, to whom, with what results?

The question, "How much should average requirements be reduced, to allow (stochastically) for intake-correlated interpersonal variations, in requirements, and for intrapersonal homeostasis?", is not, in the present state of knowledge, answerable. Answers would certainly differ - by environment, ASAG, and possibly genetic group - in as yet unknown ways. We cannot answer by the following procedure: estimate proportions undernourished if "current average intakes below current average requirements" were necessary and sufficient for undernourishment; assess proportions at risk of undernourishment on clinical evidence; then reduce requirements below the average, apparently "to allow for inter- and intrapersonal variation in requirements", until the proportion below the reduced requirement falls to the proportion at clinical risk. This leads to arbitrary, and hence unstable, cut-off points for risk - cut-off points that get amended when they classify implausible numbers of persons as undernourished. 82/

Although it is correct to reduce estimated numbers of under-nourished persons, to allow for variability (inter- or intrapersonal) of requirements correlated with variability of intakes, efforts to identify the correct proportionate reduction 83/ inevitably have, in the present state of knowledge, three defects. First, variability about average requirement is only one reason why numbers with inadequate intakes are overstated; as shown in Sections (d) and (e) above, overstatements of average requirements are at least as important. Second, the question of how many people can (and choose to) "vary" requirements (rather than activity) downward, to meet how large a shortfall for how long, is primarily 84/ biophysical and biochemical, not statistical; the basic science is as yet little understood, and what is understood is controversial. Third, the variability - of intakes, requirements, and conversion efficiency - itself varies (among persons, gene-pools, age-groups, etc.) in ways as yet largely unresearched.

*   *   *

We know that many infant and child deaths in poor countries would not happen if calorie intakes were higher relative to requirements. Some of these could be most cost-effectively prevented through better nutrition. 85/ Of this subset, some could, in turn, be efficiently prevented through higher income-per-CU.

Yet we know that current average intake norms overstate DC requirements, and that these overstatements, together with "translations" of the norms into average requirements for LDCs' lower income-groups, probably exaggerate these groups' DERs by at least 20% (see above, pp. 9-25). Interpersonal and intrapersonal variability - because people are likelier to eat less if requirements are less - further reduces requirements, and hence levels of outlay needed to avoid undernourishment; but nobody knows by how much. Prolonged and/or severe undernutrition may well be even more serious than existing assumptions indicate; 86/ MMU and/or short-period undernutrition are almost certainly less serious. It therefore makes sense, especially with 70-85% of poor people's outlay and income used to obtain food, to define an "ultra-poverty" income or outlay, such that groups of persons below it probably face significant risk from undernutrition; but to recognise other groups, above the ultra-poverty standard but below existing "poverty lines", as having levels of food intake that - while usually signifying some hunger, tedious diets and major non-food deprivation - do not, in general, carry risk to physical or mental health.

It is not helpful to blur these two groups; they have different problems and needs. At a seminar on population in New Delhi in December 1982, India's leading nutritionist is reported to have claimed: "Of the 23 m. children expected to be born in India in 1983, only 3 m. may grow into healthy adults. Serious malnutrition in childhood will kill 4 m. ... 16 m. will be deformed, mentally and physically ... [G]rowing malnutrition ... will eventually produce a race of inferior people unless the Government takes urgent measures to contain it ... [M]ore than half the children under five suffer from malnutrition" (Gopalan, 1982). Such reported claims greatly exaggerate a problem that is bad enough anyway. Probably 15-20% 87/ of current new-born children in India are likely to die before the age of 20. Poverty-induced malnutrition may well be responsible, in part, for one-third of these deaths, but will play the main, or the most cheaply preventable, part in perhaps one in eight. Typically 2-3% of Indian surveyed child populations present with life-threatening nutritional states (kwashiorkor or marasmus) (National Institute of Nutrition, Hyderabad, Annual Reports; Cassen, 1978, p. 92), and at most 20% are in households whose poverty carries the risk of a degree of undernutrition that threatens health or mental or physical development. In part II, we ask whether the behavioral evidence suggests that the poorest are at identifiably greater nutritional risk than the poor, and act accordingly.

III. NUTRITION BEHAVIOR: HOW POOR AND POOREST DIFFER

We have summarised evidence - far from scientifically conclusive, but clear in direction - that:
- severe anthropometric shortfall in under-fives probably does, but MMU probably does not, affect school performance, physical work capacity, and mortality;
- recommended average caloric intakes for developing countries substantially exceed the product of average body-weight and DERs, especially for low-income groups;
- persons below average intake are likely also to be below average DERs; and
- on a given day, low intake may be met by downward adjustments of calories needed to discharge necessary functions (increased conversion efficiency).

For these reasons - especially the last - Sukhatme suggests that the numbers at significant risk of undernutrition equal, roughly, the numbers ingesting below 80% of average DER per kg. for their ASAG (though not all the individuals in either group are also in the other: Sukhatme, 1978, 1981). We term "ultra-poor" those who, although spending over 70-80 percent of outlay on food, cannot afford this level of caloric intake. (Normally 80% of outlay is used here; scaling down towards 70% would be justified to the extent that food became cheaper relative to other needs - shelter, clothing, cooking or heating materials.) We term "poor" those able to afford 80%, but not 100% of requirements; these will often be hungry, illiterate, etc. for want of income but very seldom at nutritional risk to health or performance.

Not all the ultra-poor are undernourished (p.55). Sukhatme implies that a higher proportion of Indians, 10-15 percent, show sufficient anthropometric short-fall to be considered at nutritional risk. 88/ Yet some 15-20 percent of Indians would be classified as ultra-poor in a normal year (see p. 37). We here retain the "two 80%s" classification of ultra-poverty (80% of outlay on food and intakes below 80% of ASAG caloric requirements), though it leads to a rather high figure for "ultra-poor" Indians. Partly this is to allow for the possible need of India's ultra-poor, if they do avoid nutritional risk to health, to accept nutritional risk to performance, e.g. via possibly undesirable downward adjustments in activity levels, especially play among children (Taylor and Beaton, 1980). Partly it is to leave a margin to avoid health risk in bad seasons or years - see pp. 55-56 below.

The link between being "ultra-poor" and having too little outlay to afford enough calories" is probabilistic. "Numbers at significant risk of poverty-induced undernourishment" are best estimated by "numbers of ultra-poor"; the large majority - perhaps 90 percent - of each group, but certainly not all, are members of the other. In particular, to diagnose an individual's risk of PEM by measuring his income or outlay would be absurd! Some of the poor will have energy requirements in excess of the cheap calories purchasable for 80% of outlay, e.g. because their BMR is unusually high; some of the ultra-poor, e.g. because of unusually low BMRs, may suffer no risk of undernourishment despite adequate activity levels. Type I and Type II errors should be roughly equal at the "ultra-poverty line" where people, despite spending about 70-80% (depending on relative prices) of outlay on food, obtain below 80% of ASAG calorie requirements per kg. of body-weight.

This 80% line has wider support. FAO (1977, pp. 47-55) allows for variations by estimating, as undernourished, only numbers ingesting below 1.2 BMR - 80% of the usual 1.5 borderline. (The surprisingly high 25-30% of African and Far Eastern persons so estimated is due to (a) data for the 1972-4 years of bad harvests (ibid., p. 53); (b) application of (sensible) distribution functions to food-balance-sheet average intakes (ibid., p. 51), despite lower weights - and hence food needs - in poorer groups (pp. 14-20 above).

This 80% figure has testable implications. The great majority of the ultra-poor are, one would expect, constrained to respond to undernutrition, and/or motivated to minimise the risk, impact and effects of it. The great majority of the moderately poor are not thus constrained and are unlikely to be thus motivated. The rest of Part II first presents the evidence that the ultra-poor indeed form 10-20% of populations in most low-income countries, and enjoy substantially fewer calories per consumer-unit than the rest of the 40-70% of such populations sometimes claimed, incorrectly, to be too poor to eat enough (section (a)). Section (b) presents evidence that the ultra-poor, but not other poor people, spend close to the maximum reasonable proportion of outlay, 80% or more, on calories, and (contrary to the Engel hypothesis) tend to maintain these proportions when their outlay rises modestly - by, say, a tenth. Section (c) presents evidence that the ultra-poor eat almost entirely very cheap, especially cereal, calories, but other poor people spend significant portions of outlay - and very substantial portions of modest rises in outlay - on tastier and hence dearer calories. Each of these three findings (which apply in both the Northern Nigerian and Western Indian case-studies, as well as in many other cases) could on its own have many explanations. But together they strongly suggest that, given the different economic behavior of ultra-poor and other poor families, only the former are at serious risk of caloric deprivation.

Sections (a) to (c) incidentally provide evidence that caloric deprivation is more serious and widespread in India than in Nigeria. They also suggest (contrary to current beliefs, based on plausible but inaccurate readings of the data) that it is much more widespread and serious in rural areas than in towns.

(a) Ultra-poor are fewer and more underfed than poor

The 1971-2 Indian National Sample Survey data cover three Western States - Gujarat, Maharashtra, Rajasthan -. for which we have village studies, and in two of which Visaria disaggregated 1972-3 NSS data to which he had special access (Visaria, 1980, pp. 134-5). The NSS does not survey diets, or therefore caloric intakes, directly, but infers them from reported recent food expenditures, including those imputed by respondents to consumption from the production of family farms. However, except for some misstatements for the richest and poorest households (p. 41), the data are probably fairly reliable. 89/

The NSS groups households by monthly expenditure per person (MEP). In Table 1, we show inferred calorie expenditure for ultra-poor households (taken as being those in MEP groups where 80% of outlay - cash and self-consumed - on food will, with normal spending patterns, secure for the average household less than 80% of its caloric requirements per consumer-unit) and for poor households 80-100% of DER). The ICMR norm used is 2700 calories per adult male per day (i.e. per "consumer unit"). 90/ We use a 2100-calorie figure to approximate the 2160-calorie 80% norm, since 2100 is given in the NSS groupings. (Our averagings, norms and approximations (will otherwise slightly overstate proportions of households so poor as to be in caloric need, especially in ultra-poor groups).

Table 1 brings out major differences in consumption of calories as between ultra-poor and moderately poor. 91/ It also shows that poor households are larger than others. This is because they contain more children per adult. 92/ Although a much smaller proportion of households, and a smaller proportion of persons, is affected by income-levels so low as to induce caloric risk ("ultra-poor") than has usually been claimed, the incidence of children - the most nutritionally vulnerable - among such persons is in most countries higher than in the population at large.

Two apparent inferences from Table 1 would be wrong. First, Gujarat's rapid growth in the later 1970s probably means that it now lives and eats less badly than the figures for 1971-2 suggest. Second, rural ultra-poverty is certainly in most cases, Indian and other, more widespread than urban; the food behavior of urban and rural people clearly shows this (pp. 41-42, 46-47) and in India urban death-rates in every age group, male and female, exceed rural areas. (p. 42).

The all-India NSS data, since total sample size is much larger, permit a finer breakdown into "deficient" and "adequately nourished" households by MEP group (Table 2), where the author has applied a 2300 cals/CU daily norm. 93/ In Table 2, the kcal intakes in the highest expenditure groups are overstated, and those in the lowest groups understated. Casual farm servants and laborers, usually from the lowest groups, were usually "counted" in full into their own households. Food bought by the richest groups was assumed to be eaten only by members of those households, although it was in fact often shared by casual farm laborers and servants. Yet these persons, usually from the poorest groups, were counted in full into their own households when food outlay per person, or per CU, by household outlay group was calculated. Hence some of the (incredibly high) 6181 cals/CU/day for the top 2.8 percent of rural persons should be deducted from these, and added to the 1493 calories attributed to the bottom 4.6 percent of persons. Some such transfer, on a smaller scale, is also probably applicable among other groups and in urban areas.

Tables 1 and 2 give a bleak picture of the concentration of undernourishment. Table 2 shows that, in each of the lowest-income groups, a small proportion gets just "enough" kcals, viz. at least 2300 per consumer unit. Thus 4.2% of rural persons apparently average only, at most, 1413 kcals per CU, 94/ and a further 8.6% average 1850, plus whatever small additions due to meals for non-attached labor when at work (divided over all household members) are appropriate. The most underfed 1.2% of urban persons allegedly average only 1197 kcals per CU; the next 4.8% average 1521; the next 3.9%, 1704; and the next 5.6%, 1844. While the very lowest figures appear suspect, the hungriest 10-15% of urban and rural Indians are at risk of clinical undernourishment. Clearly, too, a further 25-33% of urban and rural Indians, while deprived of many things, can - for about half of them do - distribute outlays so as to meet ASAG average nutritional requirements.

The 1972-3 NSS data do not show calorie levels, but cover larger and more disaggregated samples, which confirm that children are overrepresented in the MEP groups at greatest risk of severe undernutrition. Some 52% of persons in the lowest four income-per-head groups in rural areas are children, as against 44% in all groups, and the proportion steadily declines as income-per-head increases. This also applies in urban areas, where the corresponding proportions are 49% and 39%. 95/ Hence, among the families able to afford fewest calories per consumer-unit, there are concentrated precisely those persons - viz. children - likeliest to suffer permanently from a given proportionate kcal shortfall. Most of these children suffer not wasting but stunting, which probably is less harmful (Seckler, 1980); and in undernourished households, there is only rather limited evidence that children are more severely underfed than "average" family members in India (although, at least in Calcutta, their access to net nutritional benefits from extra income may be relatively small). 96/ But any substantial proportionate shortfall, especially before the age of two, increases proneness to death from infection much more severely than in adults. Therefore the concentration of undernutrition in "small-child-intensive" income-groups means even more severe concentration of health damage. There is a vicious circle: high child/adult ratios cause low earning capacity per consumer unit, underfed infants, high infant and child mortality, and thus high "replacement-oriented" birth-rates - and persistently high child/adult ratios. Disaggregation confirms this picture of concentrated, rather than extensive, undernourishment in India.

First, disaggregation by States, in the large 1972-3 (27th round) NSS sample, reveals an all-India average of 72.8% of outlay on food in rural, but 64.5% in urban, areas. The highest-risk areas were presumably rural Bihar (78.1%), Assam (77.5%), Orissa (75.1%) and West Bengal (77.4%), and urban Gujarat (72.9%), and Bihar (70.4%) (Sarvekshana, Jan. 1979, p. 131).

Second, within States, there exist pockets of inferior land. Thus the famine tracts and "transitional tracts" mean that, in Maharashtra and Gujarat as a whole, the incidence of poverty and even of ultra-poverty does not change much as between households owning zero, 0-1, 1-2.5, and 2.5 acres. 97/ There are   districts in which ultra-poverty - and probably also drought risk - is likely to be concentrated.

Finally, several village studies in W. India locate extreme poverty firmly among the low-caste and tribal landless. In 15 Adivasi (scheduled tribe) villages in Gujarat in 1971, only 15% of persons (10% of households) received above Rs. 2000 per family per year, as against 58% for rural Gujarat as a whole (Government of Gujarat, 1975, Table 7).
In 1962, in Afawa village, Gujarat, monthly income per low-caste person averaged only Rs. 10.7, as against Rs.18.2 for intermediate castes and Rs. 36.5 for higher castes; four out of five low-caste households lived mainly from agricultural labor, as against none of the high-caste households (Patel, 1962, pp. 44, 58). In Ankodia village, Gujarat, in 1962 the patterns was similar (Vidyanagar and Vyas, 1969, pp. 121, 204). Average income in the lowest castes - comprising, say, 15-20% of rural populations - must have located most of them in groups at high risk of undernourishment. In Narangwal, Punjab, even after an applied nutrition program lasting over four years (1969-72), "there remained a 'hard core' group (15-25 percent) of relatively malnourished children ... mainly low-caste girls born to high-parity mothers" (Kielmann et al,,in Taylor et al., 1978, p. 3-29).

Northern Nigeria, like much of NW India, is mainly rural, and in large part uncertain in rainfall, remote, and below national average income-per-person. The best Northern Nigerian data sources on kcal intake in its social context (for 1970-71) cover six villages, three each in Sokoto and Zaria Province, the latter group with the fuller nutritional and income data. Each Zaria village has about forty usable household data sets. Dietary intake data were correctly and carefully collected, based on one-week recall (unfortunately only twice a year, so seasonal variations are not fully caught) rather than on inferences from food outlay patterns. The Nigerian requirements means are a good deal higher than the 2300 kcal/CU now used in India, partly because body-weights are higher, and partly because of longer walking requirements to, from, and among plots and water-sources: 2630 kcal/CU is used, so that the 80% cut-off is at 2104 kcals.

The message of the Indian data, of a clear and relatively small group of people with caloric intakes suggesting nutritional risk, is confirmed by the data for similarly semi-arid Nigerian villages in Table 3. This table also reveals sharp inter-village differences; thus Dan Mahawayi - though less unequal than the peri-urban village of Hanwa, and on average less poor than Doka - clearly has the most undernutrition.

In order to relate undernutrition in these Nigerian villages to "poverty" in the sense of low consumer outlay, we first deduct farm expenses from total household outlays, to obtain consumer outlays. Second, since (unlike the year-round Indian NSS) the Nigerian village data include outlay estimates only for two weeks in the year (at 6-month intervals), ten households with exceptional outlays were excluded from Table 3. 98/

Before we compare the Nigerian data with the Indian materials on the nutrition of poor and ultra-poor, though, two negative points must be made. First, in rural Zaria (unlike rural and urban India), children are not over-represented in the "underfed" groups. The ratio of under-nines to all persons, for the three villages together, was 32.8%; for households fulfilling below 80% of ASAG average kcal requirements, it was 32.0%; and for households between 80% and 100%, it was 35.7% (Simmons, 1976, p. 4). Even specific, "unusual" households in the Table 4 - e.g. those eating below 80% of ASAG average kcals/CU, yet well above average outlay per CU; or the half-dozen very poor but not under-nourished households of Doka - are not unusual in age- or sex-structure. Reports of child and infant undernutrition rates, too, do not suggest selective child deprivation at meals. Past anthropometric studies cited by Stewart 99/ report "severe" child undernutrition in 1.6% of children, and MMU in 11.7% (Katsina, Kaduna State, 1977-8); respectively 7.6% and 39.6% in a rural community near Katsina in 1977; and 4% "severe" in a Cross River State study.

Second, undernutrition seems a lower priority in Nigeria than in India, as India's lower real income-per-person would lead us to suppose. The indicators - higher kcaloric intake per kg., higher weight/height ratios, lower proportions of outlay on food, greater intra-village equality, and apparently higher income-per-person - point to a better nutritional position: all except one. Especially at early ages, the vector of age-specific death-rates (World Bank, 1980, pp. 87, 89, 110) while less reliable than in India, shows higher death risks. However, Nigeria has greater incidence (and virulence) of malaria, greater remoteness of rural areas from medical help, greater imbalance of public-sector medicine towards a curative and urban-centred approach based on hospitals, and almost certainly greater risk of water-borne infection. All this suggests that undernutrition as such may well play a minor role in this discrepancy, and in Nigeria's disappointing overall "basic needs" performance given its real income-per-person. On the other hand, seasonality of food supply, and immobility of both persons and food (especially cassava, with its short storage life) among areas, are more serious, for larger proportions of persons, in Nigeria than India, so that the relative impact of bad years or seasons may be worse, albeit upon a better average position. Moreover, any synergism between under-nutrition and low resistance to diarrheal infections would mean that Nigeria's higher infection risk renders a given degree of undernutrition more of a health hazard than it would be in India. A policy "lean" towards rural (and urban) sanitation is needed in both countries; but in India one would be troubled from a health standpoint, and in Nigeria rather less so, if it were at the expense of direct attention to undernutrition.

(b) <u>Ultra-poor, unlike other poor, maintain food/outlay ratios as outlay rises</u>

Are those households at the traditionally defined "poverty line" at health risk due to undernutrition? Their expenditure patterns - as poverty retreats - do not show it. Defining households on the "poverty line" as those with outlay just sufficient, on average, to meet the FAO/WHO average requirement of calories per person per day, Knudsen and Scandizzo find that the income elasticity of demand for <u>calories</u> among such households is only 0.35 in Bangladesh, 0.39 in Indonesia, and 0.44 in India (Knudsen and Scandizzo, 1982, p. 84). These persons - unlike those in the poorest quartile 100/, who may well be ultra-poor - raise their calorie intake by barely 40% as much as the proportionate rise in their outlay. When outlay rises 10%, they use only some 3.25% to relieve primary hunger, and the other 6.75% to improve food quality, or to buy non-food. In general, the moderately poor sharply reduce the food/outlay ratio as outlay per-person increases. The ultra-poor do not; they contravene Engel's Law.

Plainly, to observe that a person spends over 75-80% of outlay on food is not <u>sufficient</u> to infer undernutrition. Bhalla shows that "food expenditures account for over 80% of total expenditures for the bottom half of the Indian population" (Bhalla, 1980, p. 33) as a whole (though in fact - see Table 6 - "only" for 41% of rural and 3% of urban households) but he rightly puts the proportion of ultra-poor in India far lower. However, this 75-80% figure does seem a necessary minimum, below which significant poverty-related risk of dietary energy (and non-Engelian) do not occur.

We reject a higher figure, say 90%, because 20% or so of outlay for non-food essentials seems fairly non-compressible. Even the tiny group of very poorest Indians in 1960-61, spending less than Rs. 8 per person monthly, used 17.3% of it on non-food in rural areas, and 19.3% in towns (Shah, 1979, p. 26).

We reject a lower figure, say 70%, because comparison of Tables 2 and 6 (admittedly one year apart) suggests that nearly all Indian rural households which spend below 80% of outlay on food, and nearly all urban households which spend below 75%, avoid caloric undernutrition. At least one study, indeed, uses the 80% figure as a criterion of poverty (Rajaraman, cited in Bhalla, 1980, p. 9). A significantly lower food/outlay ratio than 75% could be consistent with a risk of poverty-induced energy deficiency only if food was much dearer relative to non-food than in India, or if caloric requirements per person, relative to other requirements per person, were much higher (e.g. younger, 101/ harder-worked, or heavier ASAG-specific population).

This casts grave doubt on many "poverty lines". The proportion of outlay devoted to food at the poverty line (PFPL) in urban Nigeria is taken to be only 60%. 102/ In other African countries, lower proportions have been used. In Mexico the proportion is 53% (Bergsman, 1980, p. 29; Davies, in Bussink <u>et al.</u>, 1980, p. 64), in the USA 33% (Downs, 1970, p. 7).

These differences are important, because the proportions, estimated to be at risk of undernutrition, vary substantially with the PFPL used in Nigeria, in India, and probably elsewhere (Rouis, 1980, pp. 21, 32, and Appendix 2-10; Stewart, 1980, pp. 70-71; Bhalla, 1980; Reutlinger and Alderman, 1980; Bergsman and Davies as above). Part of the differences in this PFPL may be due to different relative prices between food and non-food (Geissler and Miller, 1982), or to different needs for non-food essentials (e.g. long-distance intra-urban fares to work). However, those of us who have seen transistor radios defined as an "essential" (in towns only, of course), and used to justify an urban poverty-line for expenditure double the rural level (Lipton, 1979, Vol. 2, p. 164), may be forgiven some degree of skepticism about such explanations. 103/

A 60-65% PFPL could indicate risk of hunger, and serious deprivation, but hardly ever nutritional risk. A Mexican (or even more a US) PFPL is too low to imply poverty by Indian or Nigerian standards at all, whatever the allowance for differing prices, nonfood needs, weight or activity. PFPLs of 60% or less may indicate relative poverty, but (despite the apparent link to food outlay) have no bearing on the food-linked indicators of poverty and ultra-poverty discussed here. If any substantial group of persons is using significantly more than 25% of outlay (as always, including imputed outlay for items produced and consumed by the family) for non-food over a long period - a year or more - one should be sceptical that such persons are ultra-poor, i.e. forced by poverty to ingest below 80% of ASAG caloric requirements. These families may still be poor, in the sense of being restricted to the bare essentials among non-foods. However, they could be ultra-poor only if addiction (e.g. to cigarettes) or misinformation (e.g. about the value of costly advertised calories) led them to inefficient conversions of cash into calories. 104/

Among the ultra-poor, severity of pressure of caloric need shows up in the careful but desperately restricted structuring of non-food outlays. In peri-urban Trivandrum (Kerala), ultra-poor slum-dwellers often pawn ration-books - trading in claims on food for non-food at below-market prices - initially, but only initially, to meet hospital expenses (Gulati, 1977, p. 506). Small but significant proportions are not calorie-deficient even among the ultra-poor (Table 2). In peri-urban Poona, Maharashtra, after ultra-poor people have met minimal food costs, there is too little income left for even very modest self-built site-and-service programs without substantial subsidy (Bapat and Crook, 1979, p. 1427). In Doka (Table 4), the very poor households who managed to avoid undernutrition all featured very severe contraction of non-food outlays 105/- impossible for some households, e.g. those with heavy obligations in rent, fares, and schooling costs.

*   *   *

So we have some idea who, statistically, can be identified as ultra-poor. How do they respond, in their food/outlay ratios, to small increases in income or outlay per person? For India, including the three States we look at in more detail, the 1972-3 NSS (Round 27) has good data, based on large rural and urban samples 106/, on the composition of rural and urban outlays in each MEP class. Table 6 shows the proportion of outlay, in various MEP groups, devoted to poor people's foods (cereals and cereal substitutes), other foods, and non-foods.

Table 6 shows, first, that 41% of India's rural households - but under 2% of urban - fell into MEP groups averaging food/outlay ratios above 80%. A further 35% of rural and 30% of urban households were in 75-80%-ratio MEP groups. This must reflect a greater rural incidence of poverty-induced hunger. This is not caught by caloric-intake data (Table 1), partly perhaps because these take no account of the greater rural energy requirement: for heavier (farm) work, more pregnancies, more infections, higher female work-force participation, lower unemployment, water-carrying.

Second, for the poorest 10-30% in rural areas and 5-20% in towns, Engel's Law does not operate. Their food needs are so presssing that they do not reduce the share of food in total outlay, or outlay-per-person rises. This non-reduction, whether or not (as Bhanoji Rao proposes) a useful criterion of poverty, 107/ is remarkably consistent in all urban and rural areas of Indian States, not just those shown in Table 6. 108/

Third, these two features - Engel's Law suspended for those with highest food/outlay ratios, and a higher incidence of really high ratios in rural areas - interact. For India as a whole, Engel's Law did not clearly operate for the poorest 15-25% of rural households, but only for the poorest 3-5% of urban households. Some of these figures may be too low due to "ecological fallacies", as is suggested by higher proportions prevailing in most individual States; but, as Table 6 confirms, the excess of rural over urban proportions, for whom food/outlay ratios fail to decline as outlay-per-person rises, applies consistently at State level. In conjunction with health data - urban death-rates about 60% of rural rates, infant mortality about 70% (Grawe, 1980, p. 130; Mitra, 1978, p. 223), with, in the 1960s, the latter urban advantage apparently growing (to 55% in 1974-6) (Ruzicka, 1982, pp. 20, 39) - this again suggests the greater prevalence of rural undernutrition relative to requirements. Unduly high relative allowances for urban non-food needs have tended to obscure this fact.

*   *   *

We pass now to micro-data for Northern Nigeria. Here also, as Table 7 confirms, Engel's Law applies to the less-poor sections of the rural outlay distribution, but not to the poorer sections.

Only in one of the three villages (and not significantly in all three together) is the expected relationship found for poorer households. For the less-poor households, a consistent and significant Engel relationship appears. Once again, as outlay rises, there is a small but clearly identifiable group at the bottom of the scale that has so clear a "hunger priority" as neither to lower its (kcal or expenditure) ratio of cereals and starchy roots to food, nor to lower its food/outlay ratio. Next, at slightly higher outlay levels, as outlays rise households diversify away from cereals, but still keep up their food/outlay ratio. Finally, and on the whole at outlay levels sufficient to render the risk of undernutrition very small, we reach a group of less-poor households for whom rises in outlay induce both diversification away from cereals and roots, and a reduction (à la Engel) in the ratio of food outlay to total outlay.

This distinction between the underfed poorest, the drearily-fed but probably not underfed poor, and the not-so-poor has a seasonal dimension. Graph 1 - for the three Nigerian villages - shows food intake (daily kcals per consumer unit, by households, averaged across two week-long observations six months apart), plotted against a crude indicator of stability of intake ("worse" week's kcals as a proportion of "better" week's). This measured relationship has several sources of "noise", due to the need for economy in survey methodology. 109/ Yet the graph clearly shows a relationship, though a complex one, between undernutrition and seasonal risk. Among households probably undernourished on a typical day (ingesting below about 2200 kcals/CU/day over the two survey weeks) there is a weak positive relationship between instability and the extent of household members' average daily undernourishment; 110/ these overlap strongly with the ultra-poor (Table 4). Among households at some small risk of undernourishment, typically ingesting some 2200-2750 kcals/CU/day (and overlapping strongly with other poor), there is a strong negative relationship between undernourishment and

instability. Among households with near-negligible risks of undernourishment
(above 2750 kcals/CU/day) there is <u>no significant relationship</u> between
kcals/CU and instability.

Why does this underline the "poor-poorest" distinction made, both
in the Indian State studies and in the Nigerian village surveys, by both
kcal/CU levels (pp. 36-9)and cereal/food ratios? First, for those at serious
risk in the N. Nigerian villages - the poorest and probably undernourished -
prospects of keeping that risk under control (by living off body-fat stores,
or by cutting work requirements, restoring stability) are low, whereas for
the "merely" poor and hungry these prospects are fairly good. An X% seasonal
reduction in kcal intake per CU is more serious if that intake is well below
probable DER than if it is slightly below; it is also likelier. Work peaks
for assetless laborers (the poorest and thus nutritionally most vulnerable),
scarce and dear food, and exposure to infection coincide in the late wet
season - with alarming effects on birth weight. <u>111</u>/ Second, the graph
suggests that several of the most probably undernourished households lose out
<u>because</u> of seasons of extremely low intake. Third, there is also direct
evidence for these three villages that these are seasons of high work requirements for farm laborers (Simmons, 1976, p. 51, **Table 22**, col. 3). Finally,
from Graph 1, the especially at-risk households - say the twelve in the
rectangle between the axes, the 70% instability measure, and 2750 kcals/CU/day
- seem especially likely to have no nonfarm income sources   (4 of the 12,
as against 23 of the other 108 households)(Simmons, 1976, **Tables D1-D3**) and
to contain unusually many infants and children (Simmons, 1976, **Tables L10-L12**).

These three Nigerian village data sets allow us to put outlay data
against kcals/CU by households, for two weeks in different seasons, in a way
permitting intra-village, household, variation to be separated from inter-
village variation reflecting, for example, differences in relative food
prices (<u>ibid</u>., p. 22). They are dramatically supported from Narangwal; the
seasonal upturn in child mortality - coinciding with periods of simultaneous
food scarcity and maternal fieldwork - plainly impinges most severely on the
poorest (Kielmann <u>et al</u>., 1978a, p. 39). However, such data are for small
groups, and relationships are subject to both measurement errors and to the
influence of unmeasured variables. Hence, as a rule, we use them only to
support results from larger but less "deep" samples such as the Indian NSS,
or to suggest hypotheses in conjunction with such samples.

*   *   *

Reverting to these bigger samples, three recent surveys of consumption and expenditure, reviewed by Dr. Tabor for USDA, confirm the suspension
of Engel's Law among the ultra-poor. In a big sample (3 per 1,000 households)
taken in 1974-5 in N.E. Brazil, <u>112</u>/ the average food/outlay ratio <u>113</u>/
(64.0%) is identical among the 26 percent of households with lowest total
outlay (averaging 1012 cruzeiros per year) and the next lowest <u>114</u>/ 21 percent
(averaging 1118 cruzeiros), though the ratio falls smoothly thereafter as
poverty decreases (Tabor, 1980, pp. 7, 11). In Indonesia, a similar result
was obtained from a 1976 sample of 54,000 households. <u>115</u>/ In a 1974-5 survey
of 11,733 households in Bangldesh, outlay on food <u>rose</u>, from 71.4% for the
poorest group to 77.9% of total outlay for the fifth poorest; for households
not in these five groups (i.e. outside the poorest 18% of persons), Engel's
Law applied (Goodloe and Tabor, 1979, Table 2). A (probably incomplete)
literature survey reveals - as in the Brazilian study above - this "suspension
of Engel's Law" <u>only</u> in areas where significant sub-samples of persons are
in extreme poverty. It may be hypothesised that this "suspension" largely
explains the poor fits obtained from <u>linear</u> regressions of food/outlay ratio
on income (or outlay) per CU.

(c) Ultra-poor, unlike other poor, have "basic" diets, maintained as outlay rises

As outlay-per-CU rises, ultra-poor (but not other poor) people show, not only frequent inability or unwillingness to lower food/outlay ratios, but also similar non-lowering of the share of cereals and starchy roots in food outlays and caloric intakes. More generally, the ultra-poor use rises in outlays largely as calories, rather than substituting tastier, more convenient foods for basics. Before this is shown, a related urban-rural difference should be indicated. A major part of the difference between poor people's urban and rural food/outlay ratios, absolutely and in respect of the turning-point when further rises in income activate Engel's Law, lies in the extent to which rural and urban food outlay, in different areas and at different income-levels, comprises cereals and cereal substitutes. 116/

First, the rural share of cereals in food outlay greatly exceeds the urban share: 46% as against 36% for Gujarat, 60% as against 35% for Maharashtra, and 74% as against 66% for Rajasthan. This is due partly to urban-rural gaps in income-per-person; for example, the urban-rural difference in cereal/food outlay ratios is so large in Maharashtra (Table 6) partly because Bombay's income-per-person, and hence urban dietary diversification, outstrips rural levels by more than is the case in other States. However, urban people diversify much more away from cereals than rural people even at comparable outlay-per-head, and are much more prone to increase this diversification as outlay-per-person rises. Such urban-rural differences are partly due to the lower relative prices of cereals and root crops in rural areas - especially, of course, for food farmers (or workers paid in cereals), who save on retail margins; to the readier availability of a wide range of foods in the towns; and to greater urban reliance on energy-dense (fatty) meals bought near the work-place, or supplied by non-farm employers. However, even in cities, cereals and root crops remain the cheapest major sources of kcals. The much greater propensity of urban Indians to diversify away from cheap foods, even at very low income levels. suggests that incapacity to afford kcals is relatively less important - and deprivation of other "basic needs", relatively more - than in villages. It also appears that, as outlay rises, some very poor urban (but fewer rural) Indians diversify significantly into dearer calories, both within cereals and within non-cereals, as well as from cereals to non-cereals. For the ultra-poor,   this may have more to do with meals at work, exposure to advertising, and the pressure on working mothers (as they earn extra income) to switch from breast-feeding to costly formula foods (Reutlinger and Selowsky, 1976, Ch. 2; Berg, 1973, Ch. 7) than with substantial access to discretionary income. For the moderately poor, however, it must indicate that poverty is perceived as non-threatening to nutrition, at least by comparison with the threat to other needs.

*   *   *

Table 6 shows that the average proportion of food expenditure devoted to cereals - like the food/outlay ratio - does not immediately fall, among the ultra-poor, with increasing total expenditure per person. However, it begins to fall monotonically at considerably lower expenditure levels than does the proportion of total expenditure devoted to food. While there may be several factors at work, this does suggest that the ultra-poor, in maintaining the proportion of cereals in total consumption as income rises, express more felt need for kcals than do the moderately poor, who displace cereals by tastier or more convenient foods.

How do these observations on cheap-calorie consumption affect the findings on Engel's Law: that it seems "suspended" for the poorer groups; for larger proportions of people in rural than in urban areas; and with few differences among Indian States (or even between India and selected semi-arid villages in Nigeria (Table 7))in the validity of the "suspension"? First, the "suspension" is not solely due to absolute need for more kcals, because in many places it applies to proportions of households larger than appear to suffer such deprivation; significant numbers are substituting tastier or more convenient calories for cheap cereals, even while (partly as a result of such substitution) the food/outlay ratio is not declining. Second, from the bottom to quite a long way up the income scale, demographic factors and work/rest choices may increase the requirement for kcals (to support work) at the same time as capacity to buy kcals (out of income from work); this would square with the greater range of low incomes over which Engel's Law is "suspended" in rural areas (where extra work is likelier to involve heavy extra energy requirements), and the higher child/adult ratios in the poorer Indian income and nutritional strata.

*   *   *

Do these differences between the "ultra-poor", on whom under-nutrition is concentrated, and the less-exposed "poor" - differences in kcal intake, in capacity to cut cereal/food and food/outlay ratio as outlay rises, and perhaps in exposure to seasonal effects - extend also to more general taste factors? Shah (Table 8, note)has worked out separate food spending patterns for "calorie-deficient" and "calorie-non-deficient" Indians (setting the borderline at 2300 kcals/CU/day) within each range of monthly outlay per person, by State and by rural and urban residence, for 1970-71. Table 8 suggests that the causes of apparent undernourishment 117/ are different for the poorest than for other people. Crudely, the ultra-poor are usually forced into undernourishment; the poor often, and the less-poor sometimes, choose what may be undernourishment (but what is more probably discomfort or hunger) in preference to the grinding boredom of diets dominated by the cheapest foods.

Table 8 shows that, among the poorest 14% of rural and 5% of urban households, the adequately-nourished derived smaller proportions of kcals from that food group than did the undernourished. Among almost all other outlay groups of households, poor and less-poor alike, the adequately nourished derived larger proportions of kcals from the cheapest foods than did the undernourished. In other words, if households eating below their average DER/CU and outside the poorest households spent no more on food, but structured their diets as economically - with as much stress on cereals, etc. - as the "adequately-nourished" in their MEP group, they too could overcome apparent undernourishment. Probably, they rationally choose not to do so - or to curtail requirements; or, given adaptive capacity (pp. 31-33), to tolerate low caloric intakes that look like undernourishment but in fact, involve negligible danger - in order to avoid the miserable boredom of an almost exclusively cereal diet. Low BMRs, body weights, employment, or physical effort at work enable them not to live by bread alone.

But in the poorest groups there is no such choice. As Table 8 shows, the undernourished in these households are so despite already devoting larger shares of food outlay to the cheapest foods than do the adequately nourished, in the same MEP group. It is the harsh pressure of meeting even minimal non-food needs that forces the undernourished in ultra-poor households - but only there - into their plight. Table 8 shows that, for apparently undernourished households, the proportion of kcals derived from the cheapest food sources declines significantly as outlay rises. Thus many of the "poor but not ultra-poor" and apparently undernourished households could avoid that (apparent) undernourishment by maintaining the pattern of food expenditure - with its stress on less-costly foods - that households (with similar calorie intakes per CU) were prepared to adopt in lower MEP groups. On the other hand, the adequately-nourished households more or less maintain (or even increase) the proportion of kcals from the cheapest foods as their outlay rises from ultra-poor to poor (up to about 30-40 Rs./person/month in 1970-71).

Of course the adequately-nourished need not be indifferent to dietary boredom, nor the less-poor to basic caloric needs. There may be shifts among "cheapest foods" (Group I); the adequately-nourished may well be choosing, as they move from poorest to poor MEP groups, to replace coarse grains (or roots) by rice or wheat, instead of replacing cereals and roots by other foods. In Nigeria this seems to be the case, but at the lower income-levels of India and Indonesia substitution of superior for coarse grains appears to start well up the income scale (Yeshwanth and Rajagopalan, 1964; for Indonesia, see World Bank, 1980, p. 61). It seems likely that the apparently less well nourished, outside the poorest outlay-groups, in reality have below-average kcal require-ments (pp. 25-33), enabling them without damage to use extra cash to improve the pleasantness rather than the basic energy content of their diets.

Whatever the balance among causes, the effect is dramatic. "If [undernourished rural Indian households in 1970-71] had behaved [like ade-quately-nourished households in their own MEP group, in regard to their allocation of outlay among food groups as total outlay rose], the estimate of the extent of poverty would have been reduced from 21.5% to 14.4%. A similar exercise would indicate a bigger reduction in the estimate of the extent of poverty in urban areas" (Shah, 1979, p. 10). Probably, people who start observing Engel's Law (as the ultra-poor do not), and in particular who diversify rather than increasing diets when incomes rise (as the ultra-poor do not), are not choosing to starve, but are showing that their bodily "hunger signals" are not strong enough to indicate nutritional risks. Most probably they have lower caloric requirements than observers believe. Part I suggested why.

Such reasoning is supported by Schofield's evidence. Among 40 Indian villages, the negative correlation with income-per-person was much stronger and more significant for the foodgrain/food outlay ratio than for the food/total outlay ratio; such villages, as average outlay rises, may well be concerned above all to diversify dull diets. Similarly in N. India (including Maharashtra, Rajasthan and Gujarat) 29 surveys of rice villages showed foodgrain/food outlay ratios averaging 51.9%, as against 30.6% for 39 surveys where wheat, millet or sorghum was the main staple (Schofield, 1979, pp. 72-4). Presumably this was due to tastes, and to distinct storage and cooking characteristics of the crops concerned.

Table 8 casts further light on rural-urban differences in nutrition-poverty relationships. First, in the worst-off 14% of rural (but only 5% of urban) households, the apparently undernourished, in each MEP group, obtained larger proportions of calories from the cheapest food sources than did the adequately nourished in that MEP group. Second, in the MEP ranges that appear to be on the border between moderate and severe poverty, urban households show much higher average and marginal propensity to diversify calories out of the cheapest sources. Also the 1971-2 NSS round showed that, for all outlay groups, 82.4% of rural kcals, and 71.1% of urban, came from the cheapest foods, with the rural excess considerably higher among the better-off MEP groups. But we need to know more before we can attribute the causation of apparent under-nourishment, among the urban non-poorest, as between income, prices and tastes; for "cheap" kcals may be relatively dearer, and non-food essentials may require relatively larger shares of budgets, in towns.

Yet, in Table 8, in the Rs. 15-43 MEP groups, the incidence of apparent undernourishment (compared to ASAG average needs) is considerably higher in urban than in rural areas. Doubts about this are intensified by the fact that "the poverty line expenditure level at which the recommended [kcals were consumed] for the urban areas ... was more than twice the poverty line in rural areas" (Shah, 1979, p. 9), although the excess of the urban over the rural consumer price index was only about 15% (Lipton, 1977, p. 146). Indeed, one feature of Table 8 suggests that the <u>apparent</u> excess of urban over rural undernourishment is a false impression, and that these large urban numbers are mostly due, not to the greater prevalence of low urban incomes, nor to dearer kcals (nearby, or poor-owner-farmed, rural cereals may be offset by largely-urban "fair price" shops), nor to higher urban cost of essential non-foods, but to food preferences.

In every Rs. 15-43 MEP group, the rural percentage of kcals, derived from the cheapest foods, exceeds the urban percentage by more for the underfed than for the adequately fed. For example, in the Rs. 34-43 MEP groups, the apparently undernourished in urban areas obtained 5.1% less of their kcals from the cheapest foods than in rural areas (74.2% as against 79.3%), but among adequately-nourished persons in this outlay group the urban-rural gap in reliance upon the cheapest foods was only 2.8% (80.4% as against 83.2%). Neither the urgency of non-food needs, nor the relative price of "Group 1 food" as against less basic foods and non-food, is likely to have differed much between apparently undernourished and adequately nourished within the same urban outlay group. Therefore, the greater reluctance, in towns, of the ill-nourished to follow the well-nourished within each Rs. 15-43 MEP group in adopting a cheap-food-oriented dietary pattern is almost certainly a taste factor. If so, it independently helps to explain the apparently greater incidence of undernourishment at each level of outlay in urban areas; or, rather, it suggests a lower urban ratio of <u>requirements</u>, as between "less coarse eaters" and "more adequate eaters" (within each "poor" income group), than the rural ratio.

*   *   *

Let us summarise the three "taste factors" indicating how persons ingesting below 2300 kcals/CU/day differ as between the ultra-poor and the moderately-poor. First, if among the latter, they could often get "above 2300" by adopting the same stress on the cheapest foods as do the adequately-fed <u>in their own outlay groups</u>; if among the ultra-poor, they usually lack that option. Second, if the "below 2300" moderately-poor maintained their stress on cheap kcals <u>as outlay levels rose</u> above ultra-poverty - as the adequately-nourished poor do - they could often move above 2300; the undernourished poorest lack that option. Third, some of the sub-2300 urban poor could move above 2300 by reducing, to the level of the other urban poor in their own income group, the urban-rural gap in regard to reliance on kcals from the cheapest foods; below-2300 rural poor (far more of whom are ultra-poor) lack that option. These taste factors among foods confirm the evidence from food/outlay ratios (pp. 40-43) :the ultra-poor <u>perceive</u> themselves as having spending priorities, at the margin, driven by the need for food; the moderately poor do not. This is not to deny the rationality of the moderately poor, nor to question their bitter poverty. However, it does suggest differences between the causes and treatments, both of hunger and of other components of poverty, as between poor and ultra-poor. A kcal intake below 2300/CU/day - itself a very high estimate of standard adult male's daily DER in India (fn. 27) - must be set against the evidence of Table 8 that moderately-poor persons "below 2300" stress taste factors, whereas the below-2300 ultra-poor do so much less. If the moderately-poor have energy requirements lower than the ultra-poor, then can the effort of the latter be eased? If, as income rises among the moderately-poor, those who remain "below 2300" do so because tempted away from cheap coarse grains (whereas the others maintain former dietary patterns), then should the advertisers and distributors of, for example, formula infant-foods be restrained? Certainly, such preference factors help explain the poor Engel curve fits in India. <u>118</u>/

These food preferences, however, probably reflect hidden costs of structuring one's diet differently, given one's needs. (That is, if moderately poor people make surprising food choices although apparently underfed, one should lean towards respecting their judgement that more calories are not their first need.) Thus Dr. Prodipto Roy, interpreting the Indian Applied Nutrition Survey findings, has argued that few if any major "irrationalities", impeding optimal kcal consumption for major poor groups, exist to justify expanded "nutritional education" (conversation with the author, Delhi, 1971). Hungry Indians are poor, and attempts to solve their food problems by (e.g.) persuading them to gather and cook more wild foods or vegetable tops tend to neglect collection and cooking costs. As for Hindu refusal to eat beef, Moslem refusal to eat pork, etc., even such "tastes" may do little to increase hunger. More meat-farming in South Asia would seldom constitute economic use of scarce land (and would hardly ever provide poor people with more cheap kcalories); animals not used for meat are concentrated where land with alternative uses is least scarce; high-return uses of animals in LDCs normally involve dung, dairy, and draught, even in the absence of religious constraints on meat-eating. In India and most other LDCs, it is probably only for pregnant mothers and dysenteric children that "food taboos" are a major cause of undernutrition. "Food preferences" for costlier kcals even among those below ASAG average intake minima may well reflect below-average requirements; higher conversion efficiencies (pp. 25-33); or lack of ready access to cheaper kcals, due for example, to the need to work at a certain place and time and hence to eat there. Tastes are a big element in differences in caloric intake - rural-urban, income-group, and within the region and income-group; but they do not indicate an easy path to teach the underfed to eat better.

For example, village studies suggest that differences in diet patterns between Indian Moslems and non-Moslems are "consistent with the purchasing power ... of each group". This may be less applicable in Nigeria 119/, where tastes may have a cruder, more clearly harmful effect on kcal adequacy. However, the usually-cited examples of food taboos affect products - in Lagos milk, fish, eggs, groundnuts, meat, green vegetables - likely to be minor, because costly, sources of energy for the very poor who are at nutritional risk. More important, parents of malnourished children are especially prone to buy food from street hawkers, a costly source; but, once again, this "taste" may be due to need (to eat near the place of work, or to make up for lack of cooking facilities at home) rather than choice (Stewart, 1980, p. 21).

Taste factors derived from the practice of the not-so-poor may influence visiting expert missions in constructing a basic diet. "The food items [in Botswana's urban poverty basket] are based on a survey of food preferences among trainee nurses" and every (urban) human is assumed to need an apple and an orange a day to keep poverty away! A "basic diet" in Lagos for 1978 was constructed to include 35% of outlay on meat and fish, to provide a bare 5% of kcals; in the North (Kano) meat alone was supposed to soak up 42% of dietary costs for a return of only 5% of kcals. 120/ This is the way to provide urban "poverty line" estimates at double the rural levels or higher! In 1978 "Jamal calculated the monthly cost of sufficient [kcals per caput] as varying between N8 and N21 in Kano according to the content of the diet". (Rouis, 1980, p. 21). It may be a necessary evil to infer from actual outlay patterns to outlay required to purchase an adequate diet, but the procedure is misleading if the outlay patterns of non-poor people are used.

The Nigerian village studies give a rather surprising picture of the response of the food-mix to improved levels of living. We divided the 110 households with two weeks of observations on kcal intake and outlay, and with consistent data on farm expenses (see fn. 98), into three groups.

For the 17 "probably hungry" households with kcal intakes below 80% of ASAG-specific requirements per CU, the correlation between the cheapness of kcals (purchased per shilling) and household expenditure per CU was -0.56 (significant at 2%), but for the 16 "possibly hungry" households (80-100% of average kcal requirements) the correlation is +0.11 (n.s.) and for the 77 "probably not hungry" (100% +) it is -0.53 (significant at 1%).   In this part of rural Nigeria, even the probably hungry are so concerned to reduce the monotony of their diets that they are likely to devote a good deal of any extra outlay to buying dearer calories. This does confirm that poverty-induced undernutrition is a remoter threat than in India (p. 39), but a paradox remains.

The β coefficients weaken it slightly, as they show cheapness (kcals bought per shilling) declining twice as fast, as household expenditure per CU rises, for the "probably not hungry" as for the "probably hungry" households. Graph 2 suggests that diversification towards tastier diets depends on rising capacity to spend, not on declining hunger; for the household-wise observations, on kcal intake per CU and the cheapness of kcals (quantity obtained per shilling), show no significant relationship for any village or income-group. Again, they may confirm that in rural Northern Nigeria - unlike India - even the poorest are mostly at sufficiently low risk relative to requirements (and/or facing nutritional hazards due much less to inadequate diet than to infections and parasites) that they use much of their extra outlay to vary the diet rather than to buy more energy.

IV. VARIABLE ACCESS TO FOOD

(a) <u>Intra-household maldistribution may worsen impact of poverty on undernutrition</u>

Two further issues seriously complicate the links between under-nutrition and poverty. On pp. 55-7 we consider the extent to which the 'peaky' distribution of hunger over time - seasonally and in the life-cycle - may worsen its impact. First we review the evidence that undernutrition, and even high death-rates, in poor families are caused partly by discrimination within the household. The claim is that, while some household members - typically adult males - get more food than they "need", others (women, children, and especially girls aged 0-4) are underfed.

The evidence suggests three comments upon this claim. First, there are disproportionately many under-fives, and possibly women, in families too poor to eat enough; this should not be misread as food discrimination against these groups. Second, the evidence for such food discrimination is quite strong for rural areas of Bangladesh and of <u>Northern</u> India, weak else-where in Asia, and absent or negative elsewhere - as might be expected, because in most societies it is mothers who manage the allocation of food and the run-down of stores. Third, many apparent cases of discrimination may be explicable in other ways: medically, as a response to the greater ability of underfed groups to avoid damage, or to their lower benefit from extra food; or economically, if poor families' medium-term capacity to earn and survive depends on the relative <u>overfeeding</u> of its "stronger" members; or in terms of food habits, preferences, or beliefs that, while harmful, are not in themselves discriminatory.

Infants, and children aged 1-5, are significantly over-represented in poor households (though, interestingly, not more among ultra-poor than among other poor); the Zaria findings (p. 39) are highly exceptional in this regard. 121/ Female heads of households, and women as a group, are somewhat over-represented in poorer households (Visaria, 1980, pp. 55, 60; Govt. of Botswana, 1976), as might be expected - Indian rural data show that women's expected lifetime earnings appear to be about half of men's (Rosenzweig and Schultz, 1980, p. 10). A random sample of the population, therefore, could well find worse nutrition among women and children than among adult men, and could correctly associate this with lesser poverty among men; but it would be wrong to infer that household food allocations are discriminatory in favor of men.

This effect is compounded by another. Among the poor, those "good at" coping with low dietary energy intakes are likeliest to survive to adulthood. Hence clinical inspection of poor groups reveals a much lower incidence of clinical symptoms of gross undernutrition among adults than among children. Like household samples of diet and nutrition, therefore, clinical reports at population level may create an illusion of discrimination against children within the household.

The statistics of over-representation of children among the poor, then, mean that discrimination against them is overestimated. But these statistics have their dark side. It is the user's fault if they are misread as indicating <u>discrimination</u>; they genuinely point to greater <u>hardship</u> among children. Because a child counts as fewer CUs than an adult, the higher incidence of under-fives among the ultra-poor - and hence among the undernourished - means that a larger proportion of people than of CUs suffers undernourishment.

Moreover, it is in early life that the damage done (not only via growth faltering, but also via impairment of immune response) by a given percentage shortfall in dietary energy intake below requirements is greatest, and most likely (or, some would say, least unlikely) to be irreversible later. Infection-proneness is greatest in the period from about 6 to about 18 months after birth. Then, the child has lost "passive immunity" initially acquired from the mother, but has not yet gained "active immunity" through antibodies built up during exposure to infections (Schofield, 1974).

Thus the concentration of undernutrition on under-fives increases not only the pain caused to sufferers (because "10% of CUs undernourished" means more people undernourished if each CU is, say, two children rather than one adult male), but also the lasting harm associated with such pain. The damage is especially severe for children with high birth-order 122/ - among whom it interacts with other causes of early death (in El Salvador (1968-70), infant mortality rose steadily from 61 per 1,000 for first-born children to 137 for seventh and an astonishing 427 for ninth or higher-order children (Newland, 1981, p. 39)) and/or born or breast-fed in "dangerous" seasons (Morley, 1968; McGregor, 1968; Chowdhury, Huffman and Chen, 1981; Schofield, 1979, Appendix A; Torún et al., 1981, p. 24).

Yet we cannot infer - from the fact that kcaloric deprivation among infants and children is both more and worse than among adults - that children are relatively underfed within, and by, the households to which they belong. 123/ What is the evidence on this? A 1969 survey in Calcutta showed no discrimination either against children below 5 years of age vis-à-vis adults, or in favor of boys vis-à-vis girls. These results have been replicated elsewhere in India (Bhalla, 1980, p. 42). In Tamil Nadu there was some (weak) evidence that families with small or marginal calorie deficits kept children below the age of 2 on "calorie intakes consistent with moderate malnutrition", but we have argued that evidence of harm from that state is rather weak; severe child malnutrition is usually not permitted until the family suffers "an average deficit of 40 per cent" (Chaudhuri, 1982, fn. 28) - i.e. until extreme poverty forces the terrible choice: sacrifice earning power for all, or risk the health of non-earners only.

As for Latin America, among low-income groups in Bogota, children in vulnerable age strata (aged below 2) were fed at 97-100% of requirements, while older children received considerably less (Betancourt, 1977, p. 33). In ten African village surveys from the 1950s and 1960s, pre-school children met only 80% of kcal requirements, as against a 94% figure for villagers as a whole, but intra-group variance was great and the differences were not significant (Schofield, 1979, p. 25). Moreover, many parents tend to underfeed sufferers from dysentery (wrongly regarding "less food" as a cure), and such sufferers are heavily concentrated among infants and children. Therefore, to the limited extent that parents relatively underfeed children, it is partly due to other factors than discrimination.

As for food discrimination against females, there is no evidence, except for a short period of life in some parts of Asia. In Africa, a survey in Pangani Basin, Tanzania, in the late 1960s showed girls with a weight-for-age curve as least as good as for boys, and males in all age-groups showed somewhat higher incidence of PEM than females. Parallel findings were obtained for the Mwea-Tebere settlement in Kenya (Kreysler and Schlage, 1969, pp. 116, 138-9; Korte, 1969, p. 306). In 26 African village surveys, adult females averaged 94% of weight/height norms, as against 89% for adult males. The respective proportions in 31 Latin American surveys were 101% and 93%. 124/

In rural and urban Chile in 1974, "females and children [were] discriminated against in the main meals [, but] when all meals eaten in the home are considered, the bias disappears and is, in part, reversed" (Harbert and Scandizzo, 1982, p. 23).

In South India, the Tamil Nadu Nutrition Study confirms that women have a higher ratio of caloric intake to requirements (by about 7%) than men (Chaudhuri, 1982, fn. 22). In some parts of Bangladesh and N. India, however, some evidence of food discrimination against girls aged under 4 has been found. In a large sample for 1978 in Matlab Thana, Bangladesh, the male/female caloric intake/requirements ratio, adjusted for body-weight, pregnancy, lactation and activity, was 1.08 for the age-group 0-4, 0.99 for 5-14, 1.01 for 15-44, and 1.03 for over-45s; this shows up as a substantial excess over males, both in mortality (for girls aged 1 month to 14 years) and in severe undernutrition - below 60% of Harvard weight-for age or below 80% of height-for-age - for girls aged below 5. 125/ In seventeen villages in Morinda, Punjab, in the early 1970s, similar results were found. In the Philippines, small but significant male excess intake/requirements ratios were found in household surveys in Laguna. While not all these studies reach firm conclusions on which households place girls at most excess risk, Levinson's Morinda study clearly locates them in the poorest castes, with female infant mortality at 196 per 1000 and male at 125 (Carloni, 1981, pp. 4-5). At least in rural India, these sex discrepancies do not apply to adults; if anything there were, in both 1975 and 1976, more households in which women ate adequately while men were underfed (13%) than vice versa (10%). 126/ Moreover, in Sri Lanka, the sex composition of families is statistically unrelated to the share of outlay devoted to food (Deaton, 1980, pp. 7-8) - indicating, though not proving, that sex discrimination in food availability is not very important.

Can "reasonable" medical or economic explanations be found for any residual age or sex discrimination in dietary energy supplies? Medically, data from rural Guatemala suggest that supplementary calories alone have less significant impact on anthropometric status among girls than among boys (Martorell et al., 1980, p. 225). Analysts of these data also argue that "if malnutrition retards mental development though [brain growth] ... nutritional insults would be felt more keenly by boys [, who] appear to be biologically at greater risk" (Engle, Yarborough, Townsend and Klein, 1981, p. 2). This would "justify" a higher intake/requirements ratio for boys only where severe undernutrition (such as might retard mental development) is a danger, and could help explain why such a higher ratio is found mostly in very poor areas of South Asia, and perhaps in the poorest groups there. Parents might be concentrating children's scarce food so as to maximise the medical probability of a surviving healthy and mentally developed adult - and thus upon boys, because the impact of extra food upon that probability was greater than for girls.

Clearly, however, no medical explanation for food discrimination against children as a whole is plausible. Here, a typical economic explanation runs in terms of "maintaining a source of income - however low - through allocation of sufficient food to income-earning members [even] at the cost of malnutrition among ... small children". 127/ However, in a world of certainty, it is hard to explain over-allocation of food to men while women and children go underfed: first, much of "women's work", especially water-carrying, is calorically demanding, and necessary to family survival in (probably) fairly fixed proportions to "men's work"; second, apart from need, it is usually women who control store depletion and food allocation. Indian and Bangladeshi mothers control many grain stores, and deplete them to feed themselves and their hungry children while fathers are at work, with no prospects of consultation. The inarticulateness of hungry children, and their mothers' allegedly brainwashed subservience in food matters to fathers who are out of the house for most of the day, are vastly exaggerated in many academic accounts.

However, men do gain nutritionally because a larger proportion of men's time is spent in hired work. Men are thus likelier to be fed by employers, partly perhaps to increase nutrition-linked effort. Even in poor families - where women are likelier than elsewhere to participate in the labor force, and where the proportion of participants' time comprising work done for hire is greatest due to the family's lack of productive capital or land - men's time remains likelier than women's to be spent in non-self-employed work.

Any extra male access to food obtained in this way, however, is not correctly seen as intra-household food discrimination against women. It is, rather, the result of employers' labor demand preferences for men in the package "hire and feed" - and/or of intra-household labor supply preferences to hire out male work. Such decisions may be income-orientated, discriminatory, or a mixture of both; perhaps they are related to the association of women's work with daily, casual labor, so that employers find it harder to "capture" the higher productivity (associated with providing meals at work) than with generally longer-term male employees. But, whatever the explanation, "intra-household food discrimination" is not it.

What happens in employment markets is also crucial to the most sophisticated attempt so far to explain differences between boys' and girls' survival prospects 128/ in terms of expected work and income chances, without reference to risk avoidance. Rosenzweig and Schultz show a strong relationship between sex differences in child survival and in adult employment and wage-rates. Among 1334 rural households in 1971, excess death-rates among girls were associated significantly only with (a) landlessness in the household, (b) low rainfall - presumably a rough proxy for agricultural "backwardness" and insecurity, (c) paternal non-education, and (d) a low female employment rate, or - in an alternative equation - a high sex gap in expected lifetime earnings (Rosenzweig and Schultz, 1980, Table 3). Despite (a) and (b), districts with high proportions of landless persons feature significantly lower, not higher, excesses of girls' death-rates over boys' (ibid., p. 22).

Where food - or other - discrimination against girls exists (e.g. in N. India and Bangladesh), it may thus be caused by their worse earning prospects. Indeed, the authors stress that Moslem villages and households do not show higher excess death-rates of girls over boys than would be "predicted" from the model, given the greater employment and earnings gaps between women and men that prevail in Moslem areas. As suggested above, however, this analysis transfers the quest for the lethal discrimination from food-allocation to labor-markets. If poor parents act as if they predicted lifetime earnings, and adjust accordingly, why should they adjust behavior with respect to sex-selective child survival, rather than to female labor supply? It is not plausible, in Islamic communities or elsewhere, that the reasons lie entirely on the side of demand-for-labor constraints or preferences.

Perhaps adults, especially men, need to be relatively overfed in some circumstances to counter the effects of uncertainty in labor markets. Very poor households are both at most risk of undernutrition and most dependent on income from casual hired employment. Employment uncertainties have little effect on the caloric requirements of under-fives, and less on women that on men; although women have somewhat higher unemployment rates than men, they have much lower participation rates and therefore spend a smaller proportion of time in job search (Lipton, 1983a). Moreover, the caloric requirements of household work, while often heavy, are predictable;

the caloric requirements of job search on foot (a substantial and unknown quantity, especially in slack seasons, when women tend to withdraw from the workforce) are uncertain.

Casual or seasonal employees, in particular, on many days of the year use much time and energy in moving among potential employers to seek jobs. At the start of the day it is not known how much energy they will have to to devote to job search. It will thus normally pay the family (if the search is worthwhile at all) to provide its casual employees with enough dietary energy - on the previous evening and for breakfast - to enable them (a) to move around in seach of a hiring employer, (b) if one is found, to look alert enough to induce him or her to hire them, and (c) if they are hired, to complete the work and return home. On many days, some of these kcals are unnecessary, either because job search is swiftly suc-cessful, or else because it is altogether unsuccessful. However, up to a quite large "insurance" level of consumption, the family might well maximise the probability of earning enough to feed all its members adequately this week, if, on Monday and Tuesday, some go hungry while the "uncertain" casual workers - most of them adult men - are fed more than their average daily requirements (taking together the days of rapid success, slow success, and failure in job search), so as to cut the risk that these workers do not on some days forego earnings because they do not meet conditions (a), (b) and (c) above. Such missed chances might imperil the medium-term nutrition of the whole family, including women and children, even more than does the apparent temporary undernutrition of the latter groups. In addition, the main effects of food on labor-productivity are medium-term, and might justify the survival-seeking ultra-poor in further tilting caloric intakes towards adult males, whether self-employed in food-growing or hired.

To summarise this section, it is rare to find food discrimination against adult women in intra-family food allocation; slighly less rare to find it against children as such; and least rare to find it against girls aged 0-4, though even this appears to be common only in Bangladesh and Northern India. Where such food discrimination does exist, it may often represent a desperately poor family's last resort - maximising its prospects of pulling through by feeding members most likely to earn incomes, currently or when they are older. Intervention in intra-family food distribution is probably seldom practicable; where discrimination exists, it is to labor-markets - and the power of the poor to employ their own labor, female and male, at a decent return - that one should first look. In this context, we shall con-sider below (sec. (b)) the complex seasonal interactions among female work, breastfeeding, low-fat diets, and upward fluctuations in death-rates: interactions that are especially severe for the poorest infants (Crook and Dyson, 1981, p. 154).

(b) Safety margins, fluctuations, and nutrition-linked ultra-poverty

In low-income countries, we suggest, 10-20% of people - not the 40-70% sometimes claimed - are ultra-poor, i.e. too poor to avoid risk of undernutrition. This low figure is not suggested because reduced levels of energy or learning capacity are acceptable in any country; such reasoning would indeed be "trying to solve the nutrition problem by redefining its parameters" (Mitra, 1978, p. 298). The lower figure emerges because true caloric requirements for full development are (a) on average much lower, especially in the tropics, than the 40-70% figure implies, (b) more adaptable (without harm) to shortfalls, interpersonally and intrapersonally, because food-work conversion efficiency rises, (c) often most cost-effectively reducible if we do not "plug the holes in the human nutritional bucket" - feeding bacteria, parasites, and such unwanted requirements as aborted pregnancies or long treks to fetch water - but instead "undertake the long-term effort needed to eliminate such holes" (ibid., p. 303).

We have discussed the probable lack of objective damage from low body-weights associated with MMU (pp. 15-19), and have given (pp. 40-49) evidence from food behavior that damage is also not perceived subjectively. Yet anthropometric states associated with severe undernutrition are clearly damaging, and are so perceived by the families that suffer. Then why do we suggest that even 10-20% of persons in low-income countries are ultra-poor? Of 15 LDCs surveyed in 1968-73, below 2.3% of under-fives were, on anthropometric indicators, severely undernourished in eight (including India), 3-6% in six, and 9.8% in one (Rwanda in 1971), (Bengoa and Donoso, 1977, p. 30). Later Nigerian, Indian, Thai and Philippine data show similarly low incidence (p. 39 above; ICMR, 1977; Geissler and Miller, 1982, p. 20). Even of this rather small amount of severe undernutrition in under-fives, not all is due to ultra-poverty - much is caused by food habits or anorexia during infection; and their incidence of clinical symptoms of damage is below that of even severe undernutrition (as indicated by anthropometric shortfall). Among over-fives, the latter is rarer and normally less damaging than among under-fives.

Therefore the real criticism of our 10-20% incidence of ultra-poverty may be, not that it is too low, but that it is too high. Why choose 10-20%, not 3-5%?

One obvious objection to such a very low figure is unsound. A "safety margin" in general terms is not a useful concept, for two reasons. First, if there is scarcity - of food, or income to buy it, or administration and skills to generate either - an over-high "threshold" for the proportion in ultra-poverty diverts scarce resources away from families probably damaged by undernutrition, towards families probably not so damaged. For the latter, frequently too poor to obtain adequate shelter or education (though not "ultra-poor"), it diverts scarce resources towards food from more urgent priorities. 129/ Secondly, a "safety-margin" can be harmful, if it maps people classified as MMU into obesity (Seckler, 1980). Poor and hungry communities may select, for survival, "thrifty" genotypes adapted to food scarcity. These, if fed more, may be especially prone to diabetes and perhaps other diseases of affluence (Neel, 1962). "Certain of the bio-chemical foundations [depending on genotypes responsive to changes in blood glucose level] ... may no longer be valid, but the general concept remains ... useful" (Palmour, 1978, p. 99). This is especially the case in view of recent findings about "brown fat" (fn. 62) and about the advantages for poor people in rapidly accumulating a seasonal fat store if and only if this is then decumulated in hungry seasons (Dugdale and Payne, 1977). Such findings provide ways (alternative to Neel's mechanism based on diabetes) by which "safety margins" for persons adapted non-harmfully to so-called MMU - if they mean ingesting extra food without extra energy requirements - could do more harm than good. Such persons indeed "show more obesity and associated diseases ... than would be expected from the new food intakes" (Truswell, 1982, p. 39, and his citations). This may be indirectly confirmed by the fact that, in the USA obesity is most prevalent among candidate "thrifty genotypes" now exposed to overnutrition - viz. among low socio-economic groups, and among immigrants from formerly hunger-exposed countries of South and South-east Europe (ibid., p. 403). Attainable means and distributions of height may well be similar for most human gene pools, given extra food (Miller, p. 27, in Blaxter, 1980) - but, if so-called MMU populations self-selected for efficient caloric conversion are only fed more, they are prone to become poor and fat.

* * *

There is another objection - less obvious than "safety margins" but more powerful - to the view that only 3-5% of people in low-income countries are so poor as to be at significant risk of damage due to undernutrition. Such terms as "risk of damage", indeed, partly indicate why a 3-5% figure is too low: because it is not the same persons who, at different times of survey, suffer severe undernutrition. If it were, many more people would die of the undernutrition-infection synergism; since it is not, many more than 3-5% are at risk. Micro-surveys show only that 3-5% of under-fives in LDCs fall below some critical weight or height limit when surveyed (or, rarely, at the average of seasonal or monthly weighings 130/). Substantially more than 3-5% move in and out of risky states.

This is for two reasons. First, the environment changes, seasonally and as between good and bad years and harvests. Second, the family cycle alters both the family's capacity to earn income-per-CU and its exposure to nutritional risk.

*   *   *

Suppose that, in a community, 3% of persons (and of under-fives) are on a typical day severely undernourished, viz. 4% below the weight/age and weight/height limits of severe undernourishment (and/or ingesting calories likely to leave them 4% below that limit). Seasonal and year-to-year changes alter, in two ways, the meaning of such a correct average estimate.

First, even if the 3% are the same persons always, they are not equally undernourished always. People at risk of undernutrition tend to be at greatest risk, relative to requirements, in the same hungry seasons. Then, direct nutritional risks, such as infection and dear food, interact (Schofield, 1974, and 1979), and are intensified by the greater tendency of the ultra-poor to be exposed to covariant, and relatively severe, fluctuations in rates of participation, unemployment and wages (Lipton, 1983a). The greater seasonal variations in death-rates among infants, and in the poorest groups, partly reflect such facts (Crook and Dyson, 1982, p. 154). This means that yearly averages will substantially understate the proportions and intensity of periodic severe undernutrition. Proportions with inadequate weight-for-age, with scanty breast-milk and presenting at hospital with kwashiorkor or marasmus all vary seasonally, tending to rise in the later wet season in most cases (Onchere and Sloof, 1981, pp. 43-4; Longhurst and Payne, 1981, p. 46; van Steenbergen et al., 1980; Cantrelle and Leridon, 1971; McGregor, 1970). This seasonal rise in risks for the most-exposed groups is probably related crucially to higher work requirements for - and absences from home among - working mothers who are still lactating (Kumar, 1977; Tomkins, 1979; Drasar et al., 1981, p. 108).

Second, some people - not normally at risk of a given degree of undernutrition - move into risk during unexpectedly bad seasons or years. Average estimates, unless they include such times, will altogether miss out such people from the undernourished. Since the poor are relatively unlikely either to be able to afford to carry large reserves of cash or food, or to be able to borrow - and relatively likely to rely for income on casual employment, which contracts during lean seasons and years - they are doubly exposed to fluctuating undernutrition. Indeed, those near the margin between the poor and the ultra-poor may be less equipped to stand a lean season than families accustomed to generations of ultra-poverty. This, too, may help account for the sharply fluctuating infant-mortality rates documented in the Punjab (Kielmann et al., 1978, p. 39), Bangladesh (Crook and Dyson, 1981, pp. 152-3), and elsewhere.

To the extent that seasonal and year-to-year variation in the environment "spreads out" a given average incidence of severe undernutrition over more persons 131/(because the victims change over time), it probably saves life and health. It does, however, mean that the target population, to be regarded as ultra-poor and hence at nutritional risk, is larger than such an average incidence (the "3% of persons" on p. 56) suggests. To the extent that the environmental variation, for given severely undernourished persons, concentrates risk in exceptionally severe periods, it almost certainly increases the risk to such persons, because the bounds of homeostatic adaptation (pp. 31-32) are likelier to be exceeded. In respect of both effects, the simple averaging out - or, even worse, the omission - of lean seasons or years, understates the proportions of persons affected by ultra-poverty and the risk of hunger. The concentration of under-fives among the ultra-poor (Lipton, 1983) increases the importance of both these effects.

It is impossible to estimate precisely the increase in proportions at poverty-induced nutritional risk, above 3-5% figures (p. 56), due to these seasonal factors. However, in communities where up to 20 per cent of people die before their fifth birthday and where food is plainly scarce seasonally, a substantial increase in such figures is certainly indicated. For reasons indicated above, the increase is extremely unlikely to take the figures to the 40-60% sometimes suggested, even for very poor communities. Most surveys in such communities, however, do show both capacity to buy food, and economic behavior relating to food, indicating a much severer (and structurally different) problem among the poorest 10-20 per cent of persons than among others; and these are the proportions apparently unable on average to afford even 80% of ASAG average DERs despite spending 80% or thereabouts of outlay on food.

V. SOME IMPLICATIONS FOR POLICY

In this Part, we assume a low-income country with (1) on a typical day, 2-3% of people (perhaps 3-5% of under-fives) showing severe undernutrition (by weight/height, weight/age, growth-faltering, or clinical indicators) due to poverty - these 2-3% are not the same people every day; (2) during a typical five-year period, 10-15% of people poor enough to be at substantial risk of falling into the "2-3%" group for long enough to risk signficiant damage; (3) apart from these "ultra-poor", a further 25-35% of people often poor enough to be forced into serious hunger, but not into nutritional risk, quite often; (4) some regional concentration of both poverty and risk, so that in the poorest of remote and uncertainly rainfed rural areas, the above proportions could rise respectively to (1) 5-8% (8-10% of under-fives), (2) 25-30%, and (3) 35-50%, corresponding to much lower figures in the best-favored areas.

How should such conditions - typical, if the evidence and reasoning of Parts I-III above be accepted - affect policy against poverty? Plainly, with nutritional risk so heavily concentrated on the ultra-poor 10-15%, yet with these spending at least 75-80% of outlay on food, the fight against extreme poverty is first and foremost a fight against nutritional risk. In section (a) we ask how economists and planners should use scientific evidence and data to plan that fight. In section (b) we examine whether the balance of scientific evidence - outlined in the above assumptions - shifts the policy requirements towards focus on the ultra-poor, and consider four problems (or modifications) about such a conclusion. Alternative policy packages are sketched in section (c), and a few promising types of project in section (d).

(a) Scientists, economists, and nutritional policy

Economists involved in the policy-making process are employed mainly to advise on the likely effect, upon the size and distribution of the return to resources, of alternative ways of allocating them among different uses. This compels economists to use applied-science estimates of the "engineering" relationships between combinations of resource inputs and resultant outputs.

When - as often - the basic science is understood and largely undisputed, the applied science usually produces testable, accurate and stable predictions of these "engineering" relationships, and presents no problem for economists. For example, the relationships between input levels of major plant nutrients and output of a variety of a crop - given normal, known, and dated conditions regarding soil, water, light, pest incidence, and competing and rotating crop cover - are largely agreed among biologists. Their consensus on theory enables applied agricultural scientists to predict input-output relationships, for specific crops, with known (and small) ranges of error. Economists can then use such predictions to construct production functions, to estimate factor scarcities and rewards (on neo-classical or other models of distribution), and to advise on "optimal" allocations.

However, in many circumstances, basic and applied science produce disagreements about likely engineering relationships (currently, for example, about the relationship between human caloric intakes, work, conversion, and risk of damage). Economists must still use the "best" available scientific knowledge to guide their advice on resource allocation, but what is best? They face a difficult choice. Usually, recognising their lack of expertise, they accept earlier (and formerly agreed) natural-science research results as assumptions for economic analysis. This strategy - apparently safe,

sensible and modest - often in fact feeds outdated, wrong physical assumptions
into economic policy. The standard assumptions of economists who analysed
the "green revolution" around 1965-75 typified this effect, probably with
harmful policy consequnces. 133/

     The alternative for economists is also dangerous. First, they
must read - and risk mis-selecting or misinterpreting - the relevant recent
scientific literature. Second, they must seek guidance about the controversies
from the scientists involved - and risk overvaluing the views of scientists
who happen to be more responsive and articulate. Finally, economists have
to "bite on the bullet", and - at the risk of appearing arrogant, and of
making blunders - to select the most plausible set of scientific judgements
about input-output relationships. (For each input set, such judgements
implicitly predict, for the outputs, (a) mean values and (b) distributions;
these predictions normally imply a choice among competing theories.)
Only then can economists start their economic analysis - of costs
and benefits of alternative policies affecting allocation (of inputs
and/or of command over inputs), and of risks of such policies in
face of predictive errors and/or unexpected changes in relevant variables.

     However arrogant it may seem, economists analysing poverty-lines,
characteristics of the poor, and policy implications must choose which
nutritionists to believe. In accepting yesterday's scientific consensus,
economists do not escape that choice; they merely find a way of concealing it,
while remaining professionally respectable and while avoiding the risks listed
in the last paragraph. However, they incur other serious risks of error.
For example, the consensus of nutritional science in the 1950s led many
economists - and governments advised by them - to emphasise the "protein gap"
well into the 1970s; long after theory and experiment had convinced most
leading nutritionists that extra calories, not extra protein as such, were
poor people's main unmet food need. 133/

     In deciding the groups of persons, on which the concentration of
scarce nutritional resources will yield highest returns, economists probably
have little choice but to act as judges - however imperfectly qualified
- among nutritionists' recent claims. We must beware when experts disagree.
However, a growing proportion of practising nutritionists argue that FAO/WHO
1973 average calorie requirements, and related recommendations by specific
developing-country authorities, are substantially too high; and, despite
serious initial doubts, I am convinced by the logic of their arguments.

     The "new nutrition" does not, as some rather caricaturing accounts
suggest, depend on the quite unacceptable value-judgement that levels of
activity or performance, which would be regarded as too low in the West, can
be shaded down for poor tropical people. On the contrary, the claim is that
(i) the 1973 recommended average intakes exceeded average Western requirements
for full activity and performance - that for average persons considerable
shortfalls do not produce anthropometric MMU, and that MMU, while unpleasant,
may anyway do no lasting physical or mental harm; (ii) "translations" to LDC
requirements involve further overstatement; (iii) some healthy and active
LDC populations, therefore, show substantial average "caloric deficiency" by
the old standards (Miller, 1979, p. 200); and that (iv) interpersonal and
intrapersonal variations mean that many persons below ASAG average intake
(total or per kg.) within a population are at least as far below ASAG average
requirements. Trying to assess the logic of these arguments (as an economist
must do, however arrogant it may seem), I conclude that only on (iv) is there
any substantial room for doubt. Yet only from (iv) could the question of
"shading down" standards of activity or performance for persons below average

intake arise - though serious advocates of (iv) in fact appear never to advocate this, but rest their case on benign or neutral adaptation to low intake. The main case for scaling down the 1973 recommendations rests not on (iv), 134/ but on (i), (ii) and (iii), together with evidence such as that of pp. 9-25 above.

(b) Implications of concentrated risk: ultra-poverty focus?

Economists, familiar with "diminishing marginal utility", naturally assume 135/ that extra resources to obtain food will generate most welfare if concentrated upon persons furthest below the level of outlay too low to command "enough" calories. The assumption is strengthened by the high average, and apparently non-declining marginal, propensity of the ultra-poor to use outlay to buy cheap calories (Part II above). Only if it could be shown that conversion efficiencies of resources into calories were "worse" for the extremely undernourished - in the extreme case of "triage" (Paddock, 1975), that they were too badly off to be helped at all - would the assumption be challenged.

. The balance of recent nutritional evidence and reasoning strengthens, in three ways, the usual "diminishing marginal utility" case for concentrating resource inputs on activities that benefit the very poor. First - by suggesting a fairly sharp increase in the impact on mortality, morbidity, and physical and mental performance, as undernutrition moves past a certain level of severity - the new proposals of nutritional science imply a similarly sharp increase in welfare returns, if resources can be concentrated on raising the calorie intake of groups initially below that level. Second, these new proposals, by suggesting that far fewer persons are at nutritional risk than had been believed hitherto, increase the welfare gains from "crowding" resources for nutritional improvement into the far end of the poverty spectrum. Third, by the same token, a figure of 10-15% of LDC populations at risk holds out the prospect that a realistic but real effort can end, in a few years, such under-nutrition as has really serious consequences: if indeed 70% of Indians are averaging intakes too low by 300-400 kcals/day (Reutlinger and Alderman, 1980), it would not be realistic to expect major progress quickly. If no more than the 2-4% typically counted as severely undernourished (Bengoa and Donoso, 1973) were at risk, then no major, real effort - no significant policy problem - arises in reaching them.

The immediate policy conclusion from the New Nutrition, therefore, seems to be that resources would contribute more to welfare if their benefits could be more heavily concentrated on the poorest 10-15%: much more, even, than previous advocacy of "poverty focus" had suggested. There are four possible modifications, all of which help to locate appropriate policy inter-ventions. First, to the extent that the ultra-poor are an "underclass", low marginal returns to resources controlled by them may outweigh the high marginal utility of returns enjoyed by them and converted into extra calories. Second, there may be special difficulties in reaching the ultra-poor in ways that improve their nutrition. Third, the requirements for raising ultra-poor people's caloric intake may involve different sorts of resources, or organisations, from the requirements for generating extra real income as a whole: those too hungry to work properly, for example, would need "food first" to benefit from most attempts to increase their productivity as (say) owners of assets complementary with labor. Fourth, the concentration of nutritional stress in "bad" times and seasons requires, for the ultra-poor, a response that helps them to "cope" better when times are hardest.

Sufficient "correlates of severe undernutrition" are known for us to be fairly confident that the great majority of its victims are not an underclass: they can be cost-effectively helped by measures to raise their caloric intake alongside their current and/or future productivity. High birth-order, large family size, residence in particular parts of the country (Govt. of India, 1981, p. 16 ; cf. p. 5 above), and birth at particular seasons of the year (Schofield, 1974) are among factors associated with nutritional risk, but obviously not with any "nutrition-independent" impairment, in the long term, to bodily or mental function. In the short term, some of the victims of severe undernourishment in early life may indeed have been irremediably scarred; but when and where this has been the case, and some adults have thus been tragically dumped in an underclass, there is likely to be a very high return (even in terms of extra productivity) to saving further children from a similar fate. In such areas above all, a policy of "assets or access to income for the poor" is likely to be most productive if it involves more calories for the poorest 10-15% of pregnant women, of infants, and (to permit catch-up growth) of children aged 1-5. Calculations have not been made - they are feasible, but highly sensitive to discount rates, because correction of severe child undernutrition is especially important for adult productivity; but it is not plausible that returns to investment benefiting the ultra-poor are in general so low as to outweigh the high relative welfare effect of such extra returns when - as is normally the case (pp. 40-3)- well over 75 percent of them is devoted to extra calories as such. Nevertheless, some of the ultra-poor - e.g. the disabled - require family or community care in any country; and some "development" policies may push people into such underclass groups in particular social milieux. For example, in an observant Islamic society where women can do no hired fieldwork, mechanical rice hullers can prevent them from earning altogether - unless such hullers or other socially acceptable sources of new income, are owned or controlled by the group at risk (Greeley et al., 1978).

More serious is the second problem - really a pair of twin problems.
(a) Benefits intended for poorer people tend to "trickle up" to the better-off or more powerful, whether through market action or through the State organs themselves. The effect on projects or programs aimed at the ultra-poor may well be especially bad, because the moderately-poor may well be even more eager to divert benefits from the ultra-poor than are the rich to use up moral authority in time-consuming endeavours to appropriate poor people's (often labor-intensive) resources. This may partly explain why the World Bank's genuine "poverty focus" benefited many of the poor, but few of the ultra-poor (p. 1) - an experience shared by many other programs. 136/

(b) Even if income gains reach the ultra-poor, they may do so in ways inimical to the raising of caloric intake/requirements ratios, especially for the under-fives, who are most vulnerable to nutritional stress. In remote areas, higher money income for the ultra-poor - 70-85% of it spent on food - can bid up food prices, in the short term especially (though this will reduce nutritional benefits only to the extent that the ultra-poor are net buyers of food - i.e. gain their livelihood not as farmers but as laborers). Or such income rises may be achieved by means requiring workers to ingest many more calories, whether to work or to walk in search of it. Or the extra labor income, especially for mothers, may imply worse child-care or a switch to formula foods (Kumar, 1977; Berg, 1973; Reutlinger, 1976).

The need to handle this twin problem - to steer, to the ultra-poor, project resources from which they can cost-effectively benefit; and to make it easier for the ultra-poor to convert incomes, generated by such resources, into extra calories for those at nutritional risk - conditions the "nutrition-related project recommendations" (pp. 64-70), and interacts with the third issue raised on p. 60. So far we have discussed policy implications of the "new nutrition" as if there were one thing , resources, which generated higher ratios of caloric intake to requirements, and which should "therefore" be reallocated to those needing higher ratios. On that assumption - and assuming cost-effectiveness - both the fairly sharp threshold for the major risks, and the relatively small numbers below it, strengthen the case for allocating such resources to the ultra-poor. However, the assumption is grossly over-simple. On a typical day in a low-income country, both the 10-15 percent of people at significant risk due to undernutrition, and the 2-3 percent with clinical signs of damage, can be divided into under-fives and others. Most of the "others" are working persons, for whom extra income-yielding resources of most types translate swiftly into extra caloric intake (except perhaps for some working women) and after a few months into further improved earning capacity. It is mainly, however, among under-fives that more calories - reducing the "acute" 2-3 percent on a given day, and the "chronic" 10-15 percent at risk during the years of falling into acute stress - will save lives, and will improve potential adult physical and mental performance. However, such gains (immediate for welfare, delayed for production until adolescence at least) require that ultra-poor households gain, not resources in general, but types of resources that are likely to yield incomes, increasing caloric intake - or cutting caloric wastes (infections, etc.) - for pregnant and lactating women and, especially through better weaning foods, for weaned children under five.

Working adults in the poorest groups, then, may require "food first", but normally higher incomes from any source soon achieve this. That need not be so, however, for under-fives and pregnant and lactating women, and these may need more specific types of help. Their problem (except in Northern India, Bangladesh, and a few other areas - see Part III, section (a)) is not mainly "intra-household discrimination" against them; it is their con-centration in households compelled by the imperatives of extreme poverty to focus food on earning members (, p. 50). Such imperatives lead to the diversion of extra food, too, away from the targets of feeding programs - mothers and children. This not only renders such programs disappointing and costly (Beaton and Ghasseimi, 1982); it also narrows down the prospects of success for productive activities aiming to reduce ultra-poverty - which manifests itself, in the first instance, as nutritional risk (mainly to small children). To be specific, success will depend on generating enough confi-dence, within the ultra-poor household, in the permanence of extra incomes for that household to feel it can "divert" them - without risking loss of earning-power - away from food to stregthen potential earners, towards extra calories for at-risk infants, small children, and pregnant and lactating women.

Fourth, timing of benefits can be critical. We have seen (p. 56) that fluctuations affect the poorest most. The low death-rates in Kerala - despite low average caloric intake - and Sri Lanka are linked to year-round food support (fair price shops, ration rice, two-season farming, and a seasonal reserves of cassava in the ground (Chambers, 1981; Mencher, 1980). African micro-studies link seasonal caloric positions to both medical indicators (weight, death-rates) and poverty indicators (cattle ownership, women's work) (Kumar, 1981, pp. 12-16; Schofield, 1974). Infant and child

weight has also been linked to season of birth (ibid.) and of weighing
(Kielmann et al., 1981,Ch. 3, p. 2). Bad years - in the harvest, or in respect
of strains imposed by the life-cycle, e.g. childbirth plus mother's withdrawal
from income-earning - impinge most on the poorest. Once more, household-
level food security is pinpointed, as on pp. 56-57, as a crucial outcome
if projects are to help nutrition among the ultra-poor.

On pp. 64-70, I suggest some projects and policies that ultra-poor
households might see as providing the security they need, both to encourage
them to "divert" extra income towards non-workers, and to reduce seasonal
and other sources of extreme,sudden need. Such projects and policies, to
attack the central problem of undernutrition-plus-ultra-poverty, should also
perform well by the other two criteria (pp. 60-1), i.e. should promise
adequate rates of return, and should avoid "trickle-up" or other factors
impeding conversion of returns into nutritional gains for those at risk.

(c) Types of nutrition-linked policy for the ultra-poor

Direct nutrition intervention, to reach "the hungry" or "the undernourished" rather than "the poor", has been strikingly successful in fortifying
foods cheaply, to remedy micronutrient deficiencies (Berg, 1973, passim).
However, except in small "pilot" areas, it has not done much about the main
problem, caloric shortfall. All the four problems - rate of return,
trickle-up (to those not ultra-poor, or to non-foods), non-specificity of
resources,and timing (since food reserves are scarcest in bad times) -
are serious.

General policies, e.g on land tenure, can massively affect caloric
intakes in poverty groups. Methods to predict such results, however, are
fairly primitive. Moreover, such policies are multi-purpose (and multiply
pressurized). Attempts to tailor them towards better nutritional impact
seem unlikely to succeed. If we knew enough, such policies could be
selected to avoid low returns and trickle-up, the other two problems would
remain.

"More income" for the ultra-poor - more precisely, rises in
income-per-CU outpacing food price rises and/or comprising food produced
for household consumption - is the long-run answer. Since few LDCs can
expect to achieve this quickly, however, palliatives are needed in the
short run. The scale of suffering, due to poverty-induced nutritional
risk, is at once small enough to be remediable and large enough to be
intolerable: even 10-15 percent of the populations of least-developed and
other low-income LDCs (excluding China) means 120-180 m. people.

Food supplementation, aimed to help poor people rather than at
those proved hungry, can be general or targeted, e.g. by rationing or
food stamps. In general, it requires lots of "cheap food" at somebody's
expense: if the farmer's, his production incentives suffer; if the
taxpayer's, the diversion of resources from investment to consumer subsidy
(as in Sri Lanka) becomes massive. If food supplements are targeted,
diversion 137/ is a major problem. Fair price shops in most countries
tend to reach mainly the urban not-so-poor; school meals go to families
who can afford to release children from work to school. Also, procedures
of claiming eligibility, standing in line for food, etc. militate against
the ultra-poor, who must spend most of their time working or seeking work,
and who are often ill-informed or illiterate. Such problems have, however,
sometimes been solved in some countries. Moreover, free or heavily
subsidised food may be essential to avoid undernutrition among ultra-poor
groups unable to work, such as the disabled. In general, though, returns
(costs),diversion due to non-specificity, and timing are serious problems.

Nutrition planning was until recently a popular idea, to bridge the gap between specific nutrition interventions that did little about caloric shortfall, and overall economic policies that largely ignored it. Nutrition-planning proposals ranged from a filter, managed by nutritionists and through which relevant policies would have to pass, to an aggregate program to reduce or eliminate undernutrition by a mix of national policies. There is now widespread disillusion with these ideas (Poleman, 1981, pp.53-5; Field, in McLaren (ed.), 1981). How are nutritionists, with or without economists, to get agricultural - let alone financial - authorities to listen to them? Will not the causal chains, linking specific policies to improved ratios of caloric intake to requirements among the very poor, first need more research?

There appears to be an impasse, at least for the short to medium term. The main hope of remedy lies in using new nutritional knowledge to identify projects likely to reach the ultra-poor in ways increasing caloric intake, relative to requirements, among those at risk (sec.(d)). Our guideline must remain the reorientation - for welfare and efficiency alike - of project benefits towards the nutrition of the ultra-poor.

(d) The balance among projects

Nutritional impact on the ultra-poor will usually be improved by shifting the flow of benefits, accruing from all projects, towards:
(1) Times of food scarcity, whether due to bad seasons or years, or to "bad patches" in a household's cycle of needs and capacities;
(2) Activities directly reducing output fluctuations;
(3) Cheap calorie sources, if used for domestic human consumption;
(4) Rural areas;
(5) Casual labor;
(6) Acquisition of assets by persons at nutritional risk;
(7) Benefits - earnable, controlled or enjoyed - for particular groups: children, female-headed households (perhaps), pregnant and lactating women;
(8) Reduction of undesirable caloric requirements.

1. If a group shows a 10% shortfall, on a typical day, below the average caloric intake that its ASAG requires, it is more important to raise the group's intake in the worst ten weeks or so of a year, when the shortfall could well be over 25%, than at other times, when it could be 5-6%. A major benefit from the Employment Guarantee Scheme in Maharashtra is its concentration of a "wage floor" upon seasons when little other work is available, and when food is dearer. Projects or policies implying shifts in cropping pattern or technology (including new varieties) should be scrutinized - as they seldom are - to see if they even out the flow of labor demand over the year. In general, any major rural project or policy should be examined for likely impact on the seasonal distribution of impact on caloric intake and requirement by the poorest 10-20% of persons in the affected area. 138/ It should also be counted in favour of an activity if its returns "hold up" in years of caloric scarcity, or if an ultra-poor group finds those returns relatively appropriable during unfavourable times of the life-cycle, as for example is the case with home gardens which can continue to be intensively cultivated for high caloric yields even when family members' youth, pregnancy or illness depresses an otherwise landless household's working capacities relative to its caloric requirements. It is fairly common, in benefit/cost analysis, to weight returns to poorer people relatively highly; similar upgrading of projects with more stable net current returns, especially when they accrue to the ultra-poor, is also indicated.

2.   Apart from such proposals directly to stabilise income flows
to the ultra-poor, other stabilizers can be considered to remove or
reduce their nutritional risk. (a) <u>Small-farm food storage losses</u> can
sometimes be cut from a typical 4-6% (hardly ever anything like the 30%
of prevailing mythology!) to 1-2% by small locally-produced storage
improvements; <u>139/</u> these have adequate rather than spectacular real
rates of economic return, typically 15-20%, but in <u>one-season agricultures</u>
the extra 2-3 weeks of grain supplies are likely to accrue in the depths
of the scarcity season (Boxall <u>et al.</u>, 1977). (b) <u>Emergency credits</u> to
the settled ultra-poor can be justified by their often surprisingly good
repayment record, and by the unwisdom of artificial distinction between
producer and consumer credit; while substantial interest-rate subsidy is
undesirable for familiar reasons, a large bank or producer-credit
institution should be able to use insurance and branch-banking principles
to undercut moneylenders somewhat, perhaps by working through some of
them, and to reach people in <u>temporary</u> acute need (Lipton, 1980).
(c) <u>Peaks in unwanted caloric requirements of the ultra-poor</u> - for heavy
seasonal work, or to combat seasonal infection - can sometimes be
flattened; nobody would suggest this as a main criterion of, say, health
policy, but, if other things are equal, it makes special sense to attack
an illness that imposes its strain on the ultra-poor mainly when caloric
requirements/intake ratios are already low. (d) Apart from operating on
caloric availabilities and requirements separately, <u>attempts to make them</u>
<u>covariant</u> (or less contravariant) contain hidden benefits for the very
poor. This is a hidden advantage of continuous food cropping, e.g. of
cassava, for very poor farming or farmworking families: because harvesting
and processing are so large a part of labor input, work requirements and
caloric availability tend to rise together and fall together. (e) Sometimes,
projects or policies can be so selected as to generate a larger proportion
of benefits where relatively many of the local ultra-poor are exposed to
high variability in intake/requirements ratios, e.g. in uncertainly
rainfed areas. This is in direct conflict with some policies to
stabilise <u>national</u> food output; thus India in the late 1960s sought to
do this by locating high-yielding varieties so as to raise the share of
output in reliably irrigated areas. (f) Shortfalls can be made more
predictable, e.g. by long-range forecasts of probable bad harvests or
pest attack; the problem here is that the poorest are likeliest to miss
the information, or to be unable to take precautions. (g) Finally
insurance - overt or (like share-rentals) implicit - against unpredicted
shortfalls can be provided: more easily in large countries with distinct
zones experiencing distinct climatic variations, but always at
substantial cost, with familiar risks of moral hazard, and with the
usual problems of access for the very poor.

3.   As the very poorest people get slightly less poor, they
maintain the share of outlay devoted to cheap calorie sources. They begin
to diversify diets away from those sources, with rises in outlay, at even
lower levels of economic welfare than those at which Engel's Law begins to
be observed (pp. 44-45). Hence projects producing cheap calorie sources
have high <u>potential</u> to benefit the very poorest, though only if those
people can also buy (or self-consume) those calories; very poor countries
can produce cassava to feed cattle that provide food only for rich people.
Nevertheless, even if cheap calories do not <u>necessarily</u> get to the very
poor, a project that increases the cost of the average calorie - e.g. by
switching land from cereal to animal production - is likely to harm them.
One paradox of development is that rising average income-per-person,
especially but not only if concentrated on the better-off, tends to
restructure demand, and therefore incentive-prices and supply, of foods
towards costlier calorie sources, leaving less land, etc., to grow poor
people's food, and under some circumstances raising the relative price
of such food. This long sequence is not inevitable, but even if extra

incomes are fairly widely distributed it remains a risk for some;
measures to ameliorate it are implicit, if undernutrition is not wanted
and if the overlap of the ultra-poor, those at nutritional risk, and
those specially reliant on cheap calories is as claimed in this paper.
This has major implications for programs to breed or screen high-
yielding varieties of cereals; their usual "inferior-good", cheap-calorie
characteristics are of enormous help to the underfed poor, and attempts
to breed away such characteristics in search of cooking, taste or other
"quality" is totally misguided; on the other hand, any shift of
emphasis towards root crops, millets, sorghum and maize is fully justified
(vis-à-vis further research on rice and wheat), over and above likely
returns, by likely impact on nutrition.

4.   Nutritional behaviour reveals that, perhaps counter-intuitively,
ultra-poverty is much more prevalent in rural areas (pp. 41-2, 46-8; Govt. of India
1981, p. 16). Perhaps that is why in famines the hungry move from affected areas
of the countryside, where food usually grows, to cities, where it
is less scarce. Greater seasonality of work and income (Lipton, 1983a)
aggravates the relative nutritional disadvantages created for rural people
by lower average income, remoteness, shortage of medical care and of fair
price shops, etc. Traditional rural compensations, the institutions of
mutual help, were often exaggerated, and anyway are under pressure from
both population growth and economic modernization. So concentration of
nutritional relief on cities is unlikely to be sensible; it can appear
cheaper because of earlier, dubious decisions to concentrate medical
services and food stocks there. (Indeed, the rurality of most undernutrition, and the relative efficiency of small-farm stores, indicates
urgent review of storage priorities.)

5.   Recent national and local surveys (reviewed in Lipton, 1983a)
show that "unemployment" is not a massive source of potential output as
Arthur Lewis claimed, nor a "bourgeois luxury" as Myrdal contended, nor
meaningless; it is a special problem of the very poor, higher rates
among whom are especially serious because correlated, regionally and
temporally, with lower participation and lower rewards per hour worked.
Almost by definition, both unemployment and poverty home in on families
dependent for income mainly on casual labor. Self-employed persons
can work more if prepared for a lower return (though in the slack-season
farming it may be too low for serious consideration), and workers on
long-term contracts are less likely to face dismissal unprepared. It is
casual labor that suffers most, in terms of reduced purchasing power over
food, when bad seasons or years induce or compel medium-scale farm (and
other) employers to reduce labor use. Casual, especially non-settled
labor families are thus likeliest to have children at nutritional risk
- but also, perhaps, to be hardest to reach with food or medical help.
This further strengthens the case for "employment guarantee schemes"
(Dandekar and Sathe, 1980) to provide a nutritional floor for such families.

6.   Such schemes, especially if large-scale, have limits - all,
in essence, implying decreasing cost-effectiveness as time goes by. The
schemes progressively "use up" the public works with potentially high
returns; they tend to build up assets (roads, canals, etc) yielding income
mainly for the better-off; they have very limited scope for creating
directly productive urban assets; and, most seriously, they very seldom
create lasting assets owned or controlled by ultra-poor people, either
individually or cooperatively. Once the public works are completed, and
especially as diminishing returns (to new works) increase the pressure to
dilute the employment guarantee, the poorest households again find
themselves without control of resources that provide them with food, or
purchasing power over it, on a stable or continuous basis in hard times.

Land reform is one approach to achieving this. It offers well-known political difficulties, and in the poorest and most land-scarce cases (e.g. Bangladesh) may release too little above-ceiling land to provide the landless - not just the small farmers - with significant benefits from individual or collective redistribution. (Nevertheless, much more has been achieved than is often alleged.)

A less contentious approach involves the use of rural public works and/or bank loans to create new assets, other than land, for subsequent ownership or control by the landless. India's new Rural Development Agency, explicitly seeking to correct the lack of benefits to the ultra-poor from earlier schemes for "small and marginal farmers and agricultural laborers ", includes funds for credit and other facilities to build up artisan assets for very poor families; on the model of Gujarat State's antyodaya program, potential beneficiaries are identified at village meetings from among the 5 to 10 households selected as "the poorest of the poor" (Bailur, 1983). In Bangladesh, two much smaller but interesting experiments seek to get assets with yields corresponding to producer-goods sales to farmers into the hands of the ultra-poor. The Proshika program (Wood, 1982) involves forming landless groups to borrow institutional credit, buy their own deep tubewells, and sell the irrigation water to farmers; after severe initial setbacks, many of the problems of repayment, managerial quality, subversion by large farmers, etc. are being overcome. Analogous remarks apply to assorted programs in Bangladesh (Greeley, 1982) for joint ownership, by landless rural women, of the rice hullers that would otherwise displace their (labor) incomes from mortar-and-pestle custom hulling.

Such programs indeed address the basic problem of providing the ultra-poor with direct control over sources of income to buy food, and thus helping them to control risk and variability for themselves. At pilot level and with very large administrative inputs, schemes for institutional or cooperative asset ownership by the poorest clearly can and do work. Whether they are feasibly replicable on a large scale remains to be seen. In the meantime, the same objective may be achieved via individual ownership of highly divisible, small-scale, labor-intensive assets, if attainable under circumstances where it does not pay the less-poor to control such assets themselves; hand-pumps in Bangladesh, used to irrigate about 0.6 acres yearly, are typical. In such cases choice of technology, and in some cases credit, can be crucial (Howes, 1982).

7. If income gains are to be tied even more closely to nutritional risk reduction, one should perhaps seek the concentration of such gains - or of control over assets yielding them - upon those ultra-poor households with at-risk demographic structures: i.e., among the poorest, on big families, on families with probably high incidence of pregnancies and lactations and children under five, on households with high dependency ratios, and perhaps in some circumstances on female-headed households. An analogous policy goal is to concentrate intra-household resources on persons at risk, or on those who directly control (and can increase) such persons' food supplies - in practice, on mothers.

This sounds splendid, but at second glance seems quite impracticable. Public institutions cannot intervene in intra-family food distribution. Nor is it obvious how access to food (or income or assets that improve nutrition) can be concentrated on households with particular structures; even if it were, if decision procedures in such households continue to steer food away from persons at greatest risk, will such concentration help? A third look, however, suggest these objections may be rather unimaginative. In most societies, there are types of income source controlled mainly by women and even children (though hardly ever by very small children). Improvements in net returns upon backyard poultry, high-calorie crops for small home gardens, or even grain stores (since women directly control run-down in most cases) could have especially desirable effects. More generally, certain sorts of production are especially likely to be manageable by mothers at home. It does not follow that they will control extra income from such products, or be able to use it in more "nutritious" ways than other income is used in the household; however, if such working assumptions do seem plausible - if neither patriarchy nor fungibility is absolute - then a strong presumption, concealed by current methods of project evaluation, exists in favor of such projects.

A related approach is to select projects helping, or providing incentives, to poor families to avoid the build-up of demographic or life-cycle pressures that tip the balance towards ultra-poverty or even overt nutritional damage. This is no place to rehearse the arguments about how to deliver family-planning services (or motivations) to the poorest, except to recall the difficulty that such people are usually behaving rationally in having many children despite, or because of, high infant mortality (Cassen, 1978). However, one important new feature is the strong case for seasonal adaptation of family planning advice and services (and perhaps incentives). This could reduce the proportion of ultra-poor children conceived at times such that nutritional stresses - i.e. more hungry or infection-prone seasons - affect (a) mothers at critical stages of the pregnancy, (b) children at 6-18 months, "caught" between loss of passive and acquisition of active immunity (Schofield, 1974).

Another approach to steering nutritional benefits towards pre-school children in need - and towards preganant or lactating women - is to increase the weighting, in social benefit/cost analysis, of net benefits for the poor. Such benefits typically accrue to (1) bigger households - increasing the welfare effect because $X is associated with more expected welfare if shared among more people, (2) households with a larger proportion of children under five - who have above average (i) likelihood of long-term benefit from more calories now, (ii) life ahead of them (even disregarding (iii)) to enjoy any given long-term benefit, and (iii) chance that extra calories prolong life expectancy, (3) women with a bigger "risk" both of pregnancy and lactation, and per pregnancy. The impact of (2) is much increased if beneficiaries are ultra-poor and thus at significant risk of nutritional shortfall. The best way to reach at-risk under-fives is to direct project benefits towards ultra-poor households, or perhaps areas where they are concentrated. In these households, such children (and the mothers on whom their nutrition partly depends) are a larger proportion of larger households, and are at greater: risk of more enduring harm from poverty-induced undernutrition.

8. Finally, are there projects or policies to reduce unwanted caloric requirements for the ultra-poor, or in non-malign ways to improve their conversion efficiency of intakes into requirements? Here we come to perhaps the most promising, intellectually exciting, politically (though not academically) non-controversial, yet paradoxically neglected set of policy prospects for reducing the incidence of poverty-related undernutrition. Three types of variation are involved: in circumstances, in human physical behavior and capacities, and in adaptation.

Circumstances expose ultra-poor families to widely differing types, timings, and intra-family distributions of "unwanted" nutritional requirements due to illness (see pp. 64-5 for policy implications) and to heavy work.

Consolidation of plots, or provision of water nearer the household, significantly reduces time and effort at work, and increases the prospects for food transfer from workers to, for example, infants. So, in a different way, can forms of technical change that reduce effort, without reducing working-time (and thus demand for hired labor): improved farm implements, often based on the wheel - e.g. in lift irrigation or rotary weeding - or on simple levered or geared devices, offer promising approaches. Further possibilities exist through spreading the seasonal peak of caloric work requirements, or bringing it nearer to the peak of availabilities. As a minimum, food saving via lower requirements for effort (or extra food needs via higher ones) should be evaluated in rate-of-return estimates; better still, higher values should be attached to changes in nutritional outcomes, due to project-linked changing incidences of work or illness, which alter ratios of caloric intakes to requirements among the ultra-poor.

What of the variations among persons in the caloric requirements to do given tasks, and in the capacity to reduce such requirements without damage when food is scarce? Big variations exist: possibly in BMR, certainly in calories-to-work (and ergonomic work-to-performance) conversion efficiency above BMR. Ultra-poor people also vary in their choices between long work and hard work (in respect of both hours per day and days per year), and in the timing and composition of meals. "Improvements" in any of these respects - even if initially felt mainly by adult workers - should indirectly assist food diversion towards at-risk infants, and their pregnant or lactating mothers even if not working. Hints are coming in - in part, strangely enough, from research into two groups physically far removed from the problems of the undernourished, viz. athletes and the obese - that choices in all these matters may significantly affect the efficiency with which hungry people use scarce dietary energy. For example, given their work output, obese dieters appear to be satisfied with fewer calories and to lose weight faster if many small snacks, rather than few big meals, are eaten. Again, a few hours of intense effort (e.g. agricultural peak activity, especially in humid heat) may raise BMR substantially (15-25%) for up to 15 hours afterwards, which would raise calorie requirements by 10-20%.

It is unlikely that many ultra-poor people can afford to work so inefficiently, or to time work and meals so badly, as to incur severe waste. However, such possibilities should be researched (this is beginning: see Batliwala, 1982). Also, the advantages of agricultural projects that place labor requirements in slack seasons, allowing them to be spread over long days or weeks rather than involving intense work, may be considerable. It is the poorest workers who may be "given", by such adaptations, a lower BMR, a higher tolerance for temporary shortfalls, and therefore capacity to divert more calories to their vulnerable children.

There is a wide range of alternatives - in project selection, design, and management, and in policies - with major nutritional impact on the ultra-poor. Perhaps the main single implication of this paper is that, for all major activities, a nutritional assessment of likely outcomes for the ultra-poor
    - would, if carried through from identification via design and appraisal to evaluation, substantially improve the impact of projects on the poorest, often at low or zero cost;
    - could usefully replace much of the current attempts at project-linked "poverty measurement";
    - should, far from involving yet another "impact statement" with

which to overload sceptical field staff, provide a genuine instrument
for redirecting project benefits in the spirit of "first things first".
Such redirection would not be spread over so many (allegedly equivalent,
if dubiously identified) "poor" people as to induce a sense of hope-
lessness.   It would home in on a much smaller - though still challengingly
large - number of persons who need those benefits to feed themselves and
their risk-prone children adequately.

ABBREVIATIONS

ASAG	age, sex and activity group
ALDR	average lifetime daily DER
AWC	adult (or adolescent) work capacity
BMR	basal metabolic rate
CHR	child height retardation
CU	consumer-unit (Lusk, adult-equivalent)
DER	dietary energy requirement
DHEW	Department of Health, Education and Welfare (USA)
FAS	food adequacy standard
HANES	Health and Nutrition Evaluation Survey (of DHEW)
ICMR	Indian Council of Medical Research
IVAIV	interpersonal variations in adjustment to intrapersonal variations (p. 31)
MEP	monthly expenditure per person
MMU	mild-to-moderate undernutrition (fn. 40)
NIN	National Institute of Nutrition (India)
NNMB	National Nutrition Monitoring Board (India)
PFPL	proportion of food in total outlay at poverty line (p. 40)
PLM	pregnancy and lactation multiplier (p. 21)
WBSWP	World Bank Staff Working Paper
WM	work multiplier (p. 24)

TABLE 1: CALORIES PER CONSUMER UNIT, "POOR" AND "POOREST": W. INDIA, 1971-72

State	Region	Population (mn.)	"ULTRA POOR"			"OTHER POOR"		
			(Percent of Households)	Percent of Population	Cals. Per Adult Male Equiv. Per Day	(Percent of Households)	Percent of Population	Cals. Per Adult Male Equiv. Per Day
Gujarat	Rural	18.5	(21.4)	24.3	1683	(21.1)	25.1	2380
Maharashtra	Rural	33.1	(16.7)	19.1	1556	(37.9)	41.1	2312
Rajasthan	Rural	21.9	(14.1)	15.7	1958	(18.9)	22.3	2446
Gujarat	Urban	7.1	(24.3)	30.7	1734	(28.6)	30.6	2396
Maharashtra	Urban	14.7	(18.3)	25.0	1588	(40.5)	42.4	2318
Rajasthan	Urban	4.1	(15.5)	18.3	1748	(26.1)	29.8	2437

Source: Calculated from National Sample Survey, 26th Round 1971-2, vol. 1 (no. 238), Government of India (Central Statistical Office), pp. 59-68, 123-132, 175-184.

Note: See text, pp. 36-37.

TABLE 2: APPARENT CALORIES DEFICIENCY BY INCOME, INDIA, 1971-72

Monthly Outlay (Rs/Person)	Percentage of rural: Households	Persons	Consumer Units	Calories Per Consumer Unit Per Day	"Calories Deficit"* Households: % of Income Group	Percentage of urban: Households	Persons	Consumer Units	Calories per Consumer % of Income Per Day	"Calories Deficit"* Households: % of Income Group
0-15	3.9	4.6	4.6	1493	91.0	0.9	1.2	1.2	1228	97.2
15-21	10.5	11.9	11.8	1957	76.3	3.7	5.2	5.1	1582	92.2
21-24	7.1	8.1	8.0	2287	57.3	3.6	4.8	4.7	1621	80.4
24-28	10.2	11.0	10.0	2431	44.1	6.2	7.8	7.7	1970	72.4
28-34	15.2	16.1	16.0	2734	28.2	10.2	13.0	12.4	2130	57.8
34-43	17.7	17.6	17.6	3127	14.8	14.9	17.6	17.5	2343	43.9
43-55	14.4	13.0	14.0	3513	7.4	15.4	16.5	16.6	2622	27.9
55-75	11.5	9.9	10.1	4016	4.0	16.9	15.4	15.5	2872	16.0
75-100	5.2	4.0	4.1	4574	1.7	11.4	8.6	8.9	3190	8.8
Over 100	4.2	2.8	2.8	6181	2.3	17.0	9.9	10.3	3750	3.9
Sample Total +	11468	61813	49198	2924	28.8	19459	91846	74130	2539	32.6

Source: Calculated from M. R. Rao, Sarvekshana, Jan. 1979, pp. 114, 117.

Notes: * below 2300 kcalories per consumer unit per day; see text.

+ total sample sizes given in percentage columns. Note that sample/population ratio for urban Indian persons is about 5 times rural ratio.

TABLE 3: KCAL INTAKES, NORTHERN NIGERIA (ZARIA), 1970-1

Village	Number of Households (compounds)	With respect to requirements per consumer-unit daily (2630):					
		Receiving below 80%		Receiving 80-100%		Receiving over 100%	
		Proportion (%)	Average Kcal Intake	Proportion (%)	Average Kcal Intake	Proportion (%)	Average Kcal Intake
Doka	40	7.5	1986	10.0	2366	82.5	3688
Dan Mahawayi	34	26.5	1964	23.5	2469	50.0	2913
Hanwa	36	13.5	1827	10.8	2401	75.7	3574
TOTAL	110	16.4	1928	14.5	2421	70.0	3464

Source: E. B. Simmons, Calorie and Protein Intakes in Three Villages of Zaria Province, May 1970-July 1971 (tables L10-L12), and Rural Household Expenditures in the Three Villages of Zaria Province (Appendix Tables D1-D3), published respectively as Samaru Miscellaneous Papers Nos. 55 and 56, Inst. for Agricultural Research, Ahmadu Bello University, Zaria, 1976. Three of the 43 compounds sampled in Doka (nos.7, 42 and 43), six of the 40 sampled in Dun Mahawayi (48, 52, 63,66, 68 and 71) and one of the 37 in Hanwa (118) are omitted here because they feature severe data inconsistencies (see p. 39 and fn. 98).

Method: Simmons reports, for each households (a) average number of persons taking a meal during each of the 2 weeks of diet survey (the 2 weeks, about 6 months apart, fell between May 1970 and July 1971), and (b) composition by age and sex at original household survey in April 1970. We estimated each household's kcals/CU by applying (b) to the numbers taking a meal in (a).

TABLE 4: OUTLAY AND KCALORIC SHORTAGE IN THREE ZARIA VILLAGES, 1970-1

Outlay range (sh./CU per week)	Doka	Dan Mahawayi	Hanwa
0-2.9	66(0.88)		
2.9-4	3(3.50), 48(3.57), 26(3.65), 82(3.70) 64(3.72), 58(3.76)	18(2.93), 34(3.61), 35(3.65)	37(3.77)
4-5	84(4.00), 22(4.53), 18(4.84), 6(4.87)	28/1(4.17), 48(4.62)	
5-6	8(5.14), 15(5.45), 67(5.66), 47/3(5.86) 61(5.92), 46(5.97)	45(5.22), 64(5.27), 30(5.64)	23(5.49), 13(5.60)
6-7	27(6.40), 29(6.46), 54(6.63), 80(6.80), 1(6.83), 68(6.88)	67(6.51), 72(6.51), 2(6.56) 66(6.99)	40(8.22), 57(6.68)
7-8	32(7.08), 47/1(7.36), 62(7.64) 77(7.70), 59(7.77)	54(7.05)	16(7.01), 14(7.03), 24(7.53), 9(7.69)
8-9	78(8.26)	82(8.20), 79(8.73), 28/2(8.85), (81.8.95)	29(8.11)
9-10	23(9.29), 44(9.34), 31(9.44)	40(9.62), 20(9.82)	5(9.08), 44(9.10), 6(9.30), 41(9.58)
10-11	25(10.24), 74(10.73), 17(10.02)	15(10.61), 31(10.84)	48(10.03), 17(10.15), 58(10.40) 74(10.01), 76(10.96), 1(10.99)
11-12	53(11.37)	78/2(11.04)	4(11.12), 31(11.13)
12-16	10(14.38)	4(12.73), 1/2(13.66), 57/3(14.10) 84(15.18)	28(12.16), 43(13.42), 12(13.45), 18(14.45)
16-20	72(16.76)	85/3(17.52), 33(19.21), 37(19.92)	25(18.82)
20-24		41(22.23)	38(21.17), 63(22.48), 36(23.01)
24-28	71/2(25.05), 7(27.02)	1/1(25.65)	72(24.36), 80(27.37)
28-32		76(31.51)	

Single underlining: 80-100% of ASAG-specific daily kcal requirements eaten.
Double underlinings: below 80%. Each unbracketed figure is a compound
(household) number; following bracketed figure is household outlay (net of farm
expenses) in sh./consumer uni t/week, averaged over 2 survey weeks about 6
months apart.

Source: As Table 3. Two households in DM (spending 2.0 nd 95.1 sh/CU/wk) and
four in Hanwa (36.9, 41.1, 45.5, 92.4) have been excluded; see p. 74. Farm
expenses: data kindly supplied by Dr. Simmons.

TABLE 5: HOUSEHOLD SIZE AND KCAL POSITION, ZARIA, 1970-71

Proportion of ASAG kcal Requirements	DOAKA		DAN MAHAWAYI		HANWA		ALL THESE	
	No. of Households	CUs per Household	No. of Households	CUs per Household	No. of Households	CUs per Household	No. of Households	CUs per Household
Below 80%	3	9.60	9	7.41	5	14.39	17	9.85
80-100%	4	9.65	7	7.51	3	9.08	14	8.46
100%	33	6.04	16	5.18	24	8.18	73	6.55

Source: As Table 3. Households exceeded as in Table 4.

TABLE 6: MONTHLY CONSUMER EXPENDITURE (RS) PER PERSON, OCT. 1972 – SEPT. 1973, INDIA

Monthly exp. per person (Rupees)	0-13	13-15	15-18	18-21	21-24	24-28	28-34	34-43	43-55	55-75	75-100	100-150	150-200	200+	All
R G u — U j															
Sample households	11	7	37	92	131	282	520	720	662	527	243	114	20	15	3381
% food exp.:															
cereals, etc.	67.2	67.2	60.0	60.4	58.7	57.0	54.1	50.8	46.9	42.7	41.2	33.1	31.9	28.8	45.6
% all exp. food	82.6	80.2	80.6	81.9	81.1	82.8	83.0	83.01	80.0	77.3	69.6	62.1	54.6	37.1	73.4
M a — R h															
Sample households	74	67	162	266	532	522	810	1051	882	656	253	124	25	25	5249
% food exp.:															
cereals, etc.	67.6	71.0	67.4	65.9	64.3	66.1	64.6	62.5	59.7	56.4	49.8	43.6	42.9	37.1	59.6
% all exp.: food	78.0	80.0	78.2	79.6	80.7	80.5	79.0	76.3	72.6	67.4	61.3	52.3	41.3	13.4	67.6
R a — a j															
Sample households	36	22	65	114	125	219	319	383	369	339	156	100	18	20	2285
% food exp.:															
cereals, etc.	78.7	73.1	76.4	69.4	72.5	68.1	63.7	60.4	51.7	46.9	42.5	37.2	22.9	25.6	50.5
% all exp.: food	84.8	88.0	83.8	84.7	87.1	84.3	83.6	81.4	78.4	72.6	69.3	67.4	68.4	49.6	73.9
I n L d i a															
Sample households	1173	941	2275	3430	4257	6873	10738	13649	11872	9311	4334	2409	621	387	72270
% food exp.:															
cereals, etc.	76.9	75.9	74.9	72.7	70.9	68.6	65.8	61.7	56.7	51.5	44.4	38.6	35.0	29.0	53.4
% all exp.: food	81.4	82.7	82.8	82.6	82.4	81.8	80.8	78.9	75.6	71.6	66.0	59.4	52.0	38.1	72.8
U G R u B A j N															
Sample households	2	–	8	6	11	53	141	311	437	474	297	166	48	36	1990
% food exp.:															
cereals, etc.	–	–	35.0	38.8	51.7	48.1	46.1	43.7	39.5	35.9	30.5	26.9	21.7	13.1	36.2
% all exp.: food	–	–	80.8	79.0	79.8	80.4	81.8	80.0	78.3	74.7	68.6	62.9	53.5	45.9	72.0

TABLE 6 (CONTINUED):   MONTHLY CONSUMER EXPENDITURE (RS) PER PERSON, OCT. 1972 - SEPT. 1973, INDIA

Monthly exp. per person (Rupees)	0-13	13-15	15-18	18-21	21-24	24-28	28-34	34-43	43-55	55-75	75-100	100-150	150-200	200+	ALL
U R M Sample households	39	22	44	75	112	246	385	699	850	1036	832	1024	413	404	6181
% food exp.: cereals, etc.	42.1	43.5	55.2	60.8	53.4	48.9	48.4	44.3	37.0	30.5	24.2	17.9	13.6	10.7	27.1
% all exp.: food	69.5	81.7	79.6	77.7	79.7	76.0	76.1	75.0	71.6	67.6	62.8	59.1	54.5	40.5	61.1
R B Sample households	7	3	17	29	45	95	190	364	428	425	321	281	97	90	2392
% food exp.: cereals, etc.	58.7	60.1	57.0	60.8	52.0	54.8	52.4	47.1	42.3	36.2	29.4	23.2	21.7	15.3	35.6
% all exp.: food	81.4	74.2	79.6	82.3	82.6	82.2	80.4	78.6	75.1	70.7	64.7	57.5	54.1	42.9	66.1
A I N Sample households	172	125	355	689	1088	2239	4475	7509	8693	9678	6955	6366	2348	2128	52820
% food exp.: cereals, etc.	63.1	62.4	60.9	60.3	59.5	56.0	53.9	49.5	43.9	37.5	30.3	23.5	17.9	13.4	36.4
% all exp.: food	75.5	79.1	80.2	80.1	79.7	78.8	78.0	76.5	73.1	68.9	63.9	58.4	52.7	38.4	64.5

Source: Sarvekshana, Jan. 1979, pp. S334, S340, S346, S355, S400, S406, S413, S423.

Notes: (1) "Cereals etc." includes "cereal substitutes" but not gram or other pulses and pulse products.

(2) Average monthly consumer outlay per person, rural: Gujarat, Rs. 51.70; Maharashtra, 41.55; Rajasthan, 51.98; all-India, 44.17. Urban: Gujarat, Rs. 57.58; Maharashtra, Rs. 74.84; Rajasthan, Rs. 63.87; all-India, RS. 63.33.

TABLE 7: CORRELATIONS OF OUTLAY ON FOOD/OUTLAY RATIOS, ZARIA

Village	Sector	r of outlay-per-person on household food/outlay ratio	Significant level
Doka	Poorer 20 households	+0.2524	N.S.
	Less-poor 20	-0.5844	1%
Dan Mahawayl	Poorer 12	-0.6388	2%
	Less-poor 20	-0.5995	1%
Hanwa	Poorer 14	+0.7080	1%
	Less-poor 18	-0.7009	0.1%
All Three	Poorer 50	-0.0911	N.S.
	Less-poor 54	-0.5854	0.1%

Source: as Table 3.

Note: cut-off points: Doka, poorer 20 have below 6.65sh/CU/week; Dan Mahawayl, poorer 12 below 7sh/CU/week; Hanwa, poorer 14 below 10sh/CU/week; for all three pooled, poorer 50 are below 8sh/CU/week.

TABLE 8: UNDERNOURISHED, OUTLAY AND DIET STRUCTURE, INDIA, 1970-71

Household outlay (Rs./month/person)	% of all households	Under 2300 kcals/CU/day			Over 2300 kcals/CU/day		
		% of outlay group	kcals. per consumer unit per day	Percentage of kcals from Food Group I	% of outlay group	kcals per consumer unit per day	Percentage of kcals from Food Group I
RURAL							
0-15	3.9	91.0	1366	91.1	9.0	2775	82.0
15-21	10.5	76.3	1727	88.7	23.7	2694	86.4
21-24	7.1	57.3	1867	86.9	42.7	2851	88.5
24-28	10.2	44.1	1928	84.5	55.9	2828	86.5
28-34	15.2	28.1	1970	82.6	71.9	3033	85.7
34-43	17.7	14.8	1999	79.3	85.2	3323	83.2
43-55	14.4	7.4	2010	74.6	92.6	3634	80.8
55-75	11.5	4.0	1913	74.6	96.0	4104	76.5
75-100	5.2	1.7	1601	79.0	98.3	4624	76.7
100+	4.2	2.3	1745	34.7	97.7	6285	66.8
All	100.0	28.8	1810	86.0	71.2	3093	81.0
URBAN							
0-15	0.9	97.2	1232	87.4	2.8	3288	76.9
15-21	3.7	92.2	1561	85.5	7.8	2966	84.0
21-24	3.6	80.4	1722	83.4	19.6	2229	86.8
24-28	16.0	72.4	1791	81.7	27.6	2439	85.3
28-34	10.2	67.8	1872	78.5	32.2	2484	82.5
34-43	14.9	43.9	1922	74.2	56.1	2672	80.4
43-55	15.4	27.9	1984	71.0	72.1	2869	74.7
55-75	16.9	16.9	2013	63.2	83.1	3036	69.3
75-100	11.3	8.8	1992	57.6	91.2	3306	62.0
100+	17.0	3.9	1879	46.4	96.1	3899	50.1
All	100.0	32.6	1840	76.7	67.4	2878	68.4

Source: C. H. Shah, "Food preferences and nutrition: a perspective on poverty", Presidential Address Indian Society of Agricultural Economics, Bangalore, Dec. 1979, pp. 28-29 (using Round 26, National Sample Survey). "Food Group I" comprises cereals, cereals substitutes, potato, sugar and jaggery (M. R. Rao, "Nutrition situation in India during 1971-72", Sarvekshana, Jan. 1979, p. 114.)

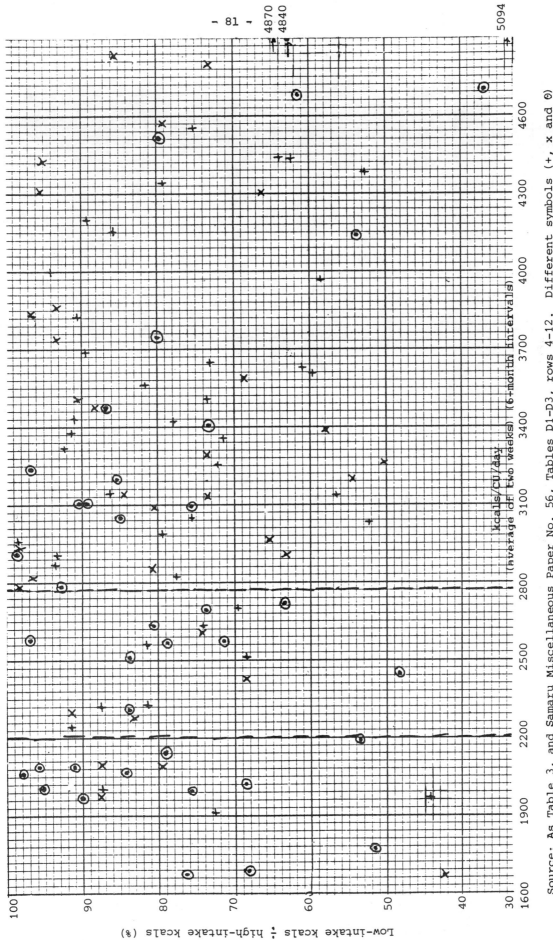

GRAPH 1: <u>RELATION OF KCAL INTAKE TO ITS STABILITY, ZARIA, 1970-71</u>

Source: As Table 3, and Samaru Miscellaneous Paper No. 56, Tables D1-D3, rows 4-12. Different symbols (+, x and ⊖) are used for households in the three different villages.

GRAPH 2: <u>ADEQUACY OF DIETARY ENERGY AND ITS COST, ZARIA, 1970-71</u>

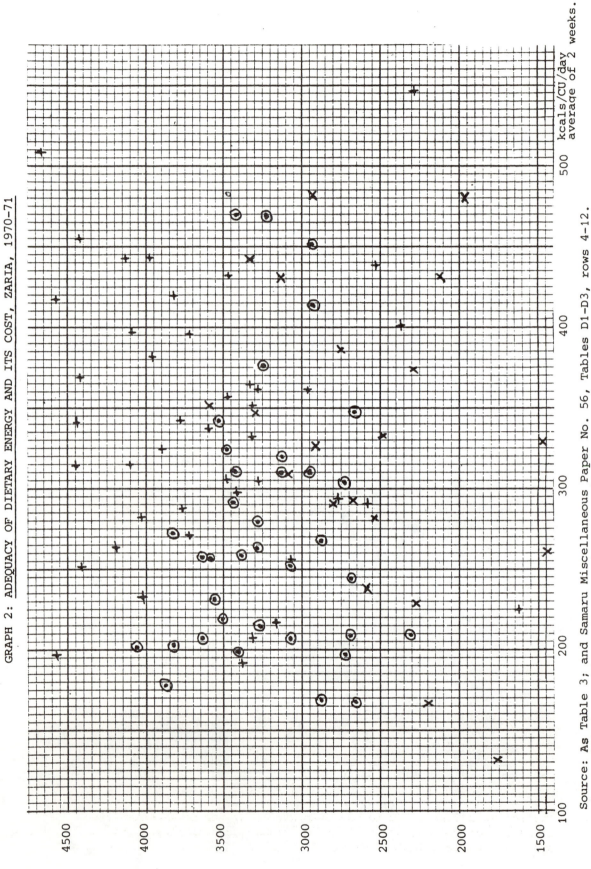

Source: As Table 3; and Samaru Miscellaneous Paper No. 56, Tables D1-D3, rows 4-12.
Different symbols (+, x and θ) are used for households in the three different villages.

FOOTNOTES

1. Sen (1981) pp. 32-8, shows how to combine "numbers" and "severity" into a single indicator of absolute lack - of income, or school places, etc.

2. An equity argument could even be made for allocating such a specific-purpose resource, not where people need it most, but where they are poorest.

3. This implausible assumption simplifies the argument, but can be dropped.

4. Equity conflicts between reducing poverty and inequality may be rather rare. On the priority of the former goals, see Rawls (1971).

5. "Primary poverty" - which is what is meant by "poverty" here - is due to insufficient resources; "secondary poverty", to inefficient allocation of adequate resources.

6. For fuller discussion see Schofield (1979), pp. 148-9.

7. Using relative prices of any one country or a composite; see Kravis et al. (1982). Thailand has similar GNP-per-person and distribution to the Philippines, but food is cheaper relative to other items, and nutrition therefore better (Geissler and Miller, 1982).

8. Outlay on addictions, possibly in the case of alcohol net of the alternative cost of buying the calories alone, should perhaps be deducted from discretionary income or outlay spendable on food.

9. Most "poverty counts" ignore the extent to which victims fall below the poverty line. See above, fn. 1.

10. The proportion of the year in poverty, and such years as a proportion of that lifetime, are beginning to be recognised as components as important as point observations.

11. Generally, they have too few "prospects" to borrow substantial amounts for long, and are too poor to have built up much by way of "dissavable" assets.

12. See below, pp. 14-19. We shall argue that only the Gomez indicators of "severe malnutrition" with respect to weight/height for adults and weight/age for children appear to correlate significantly with functional impairment.

13. See below, Sec. II, 7. This "own behavior" comprises, as income decreases, growing propensities to spend on non-food, on non-cereals within food, and on costlier cereals within cereals - none of them characteristics of the extremely poor.

14. Improved child nutrition increases early learning power, and hence lifetime earning power (Selowsky, 1980).

15. This is emphatically not to say that good fits can be expected from simple linear regression of food outlay upon total household income or outlay. See below, pp. 40-43,

16. National Institute of Nutrition (1976). Conversely, of households with enough calories in the seven States, proportions of protein-inadequates range from zero (in four) to 6.1%.

17. Sukhatme (1977). A good, quantified discussion of such an exceptional region (and a contrasting normal region) is Korte (1974); this is subsequent to FAO/WHO's 1973 reduction of protein requirements, though not to the further reductions reported in Poleman (1981).

18. Ibid.; Chitre and Agte (1978), p. 198; Dikshit and Chitre (1978), pp. 269-70.; on the chemistry of transamination, see Davidson et al., (1975), p. 58; on pellagra and leucine-tryptophan imbalance, see ibid., p. 348, and Gopalan (1969), p. 197; on the toxic factor in lathyrism, see Davidson et al., p. 274 (recent information given me at NIN, Hyderabad, stressed a probable link to leucine-isoleucine imbalance).

19. Bhalla (1980), p. 80; cf. Poleman (1981), p. 9. The US Board recommends 2,700 kcal. daily for men, and 2000 for women, in this group, but the reference weights are respectively 70 kg. and 58 kg. As recently as 1958 the respective recommendations were 3200 and 2300, respectively 19% and 15% higher.

20. DHEW (1979), p. 2 explains that "cell mass tends to decrease with age even as weight increases, so allowances tend to overstate the nutrient needs of older people as compared with younger"; at least for energy needs, the last four words quoted can logically be removed.

21. For similar reasons, significant cuts in dietary energy requirements elsewhere (Buss, 1979; Mohan et al., 1981, pp. 16-17) are probably too small - though this remains contentious.

22. DHEW (1979), p. 1-1 and 1-2. This supports our suspicion (p. 13) that HANES - and FAO/WHO - set particularly high DERs for older people (despite their falling cell mass).

23. Gersovitz et al. (1978), pp. 48-55; Tilve (1978), p. 6. "Talking a good diet", at low intake levels, outweighs the effect of concealment and forgetfulness.

24. A 10% reduction in FAO/WHO energy requirements reduces estimated numbers in kcal deficit by over a quarter: Reutlinger and Alderman (1980), p. 15. Compare Bhalla (1980), p. 84, and Mohan et al. (1981), p. 8. Sen's indicator of severity of poverty - headcount (viz. proportion of persons below poverty line) times their average proportionate shortfall, whether or not modified to allow for inequality among the poor - is much less sensitive to specification error (e.g. of caloric requirement or of income needed to buy it) than is head-count alone.

25. (a) See pp. 25-34. Because intakes are positively correlated with requirements (given income), and because conversion efficiency of food into work rises when intake falls, this is not offset by the presence of above-average intakes and requirements on other days (Sukhatme, Srinivasan); (b) ICMR and the Indian National Nutrition Monitoring Board (NNMB) do not make this error.

26. It is not, however, really "safe" (a) to allocate scarce resources, away from the undernourished, to increase caloric intakes of those whose need is small or absent, (b) to risk making the latter overweight, c) to settle people into high caloric intake levels unsustainable without undue sacrifice of other goals or needs.

27. NNMB (1981), pp. 25-40, for weights (averaged for eight States across the four age-groups 20-25, 25-30, 30-35 and 35-40; after age 29, weight gain is fat only and hence unhelpful); pp. 7, 9 for ICMR's DERs; FAO/WHO (1973) p. 31, for theirs; fn. 19 above for the US (1980) DER, here scaled down for body-weight ratio (49.1/70), but refering to moderately active workers (as against ICMR's sedentary tropical reference) and demonstrably still too high even for the USA. For sedentary adult male workers, even at ICMR's 55 kg reference weight (instead of 49.1 kg actual), FAO/WHO gives 2310 kcals (not 2400), and US (1980) gives 2162. Chaudhuri (1982), fn. 15, cites NIN and ICMR work from 1977 showing the same (2400) figure.

28. For adult males, ICMR assigns "moderate" workers 1.2 times the DER (per kg body weight), as sedentary workers (FAO/WHO, 1.095), and heavy workers 1.6 times (FAO/WHO, 1.286, or 1.476 for "exceptionally heavy" work). Adult female sedentary workers, averaging 42.0 kg in India, for ICMR require 0.8 times the DER for a 49.1 kg sedentary male worker (FAO/WHO, 0.733); at these weights, adult females require 0.9 times the sedentary adult male level, according to ICMR, if they do moderate work (FAO/WHO, 0.814); and with heavy work 1.2 times (FAO/WHO, 0.957, or 1.120 for "exceptionally heavy" work).

29. Devadas et al. (1979), p. 437. As against ICMR's influential DER of 2400 kcal.person/day at "mouth level" per (sedentary adult male) CU, Sukhatme's figure of 2300 at retail level - presumably about 2100 in the mouth - is also widely accepted; cf. Rao (1979), p. 112. See, however, fns. 27 and 28 above, implying even lower DERs.

30. See above, fn. 28; and compare FAO/WHO (1973), p. 31, with the much higher requirements implicit in ICMR standards as cited by Bang (1981), p. 1419.

31. Ebrahim (1979), pp. 29, 32. 34. Actually 27,533, assuming each trimester is 280/3 days.

32. On the 42 kg average body weight for Indian rural women in 1980 as found by the NNMB, see fn. 28; it would imply 42/55 of Ebrahim's 27,550 kcal requirements, viz. 21,050. Yet the ICMR figure (88,200) for a 280-day pregnancy is implied by their per-kg requirements of 7 per day, at a 55 kg reference weight, for a 280-day pregnancy (Ebrahim, 1979, p. 32).

33. For a gloomy reading of the pregnancy stress of Nigerian women (largely invalidated if Ebrahim is correct) see Harrington (1982). See also Whitehead (1981).

34. Kwashiorkor typically affects below 1% of Indian under-fives, marasmus 2.4%, and severe anthropometric undernutrition (below 60% of Harvard median weight-for-age) some 8-10% (Chaudhuri, 1982, fns. 25-27, 30). See also p. 58.

35. Petrasek (1978), p. 510. His supporting evidence (citing Consolazio) also relates to the extra requirements of acclimatization to very heavy work in hot climates; the greater food-work conversion efficiency and lower BMR, usually associated with acclimatized tropical populations at normal work levels, are not challenged, but are confirmed by his citations of Edholm.

36. Seckler (1980), p. 27; by age 18, healthy Indian boys from the top socio-economic group averaged 84% of Harvard weight-for-age, from the third 79%, from the lowest (sixth) group 73%.

37. Averaged over a 4½-year study, as compared with control villages, "nutrition care" made surprisingly little (though statistically significant) difference to weight-age ratios in the rural Punjab. For example, among 21-month-old children, the ratio was 74% of the Harvard standard in the control villages, 76% in villages with nutrition care only, and 77% with both nutrition and medical care; at 31 months, the respective proportions were 74%, 77% and 78%. Taylor et al., (1978), p. 14.

38. National Institute of Nutrition (1978), pp. 139-142 (the text stresses other issues; those stressed here rely on Table 84.) AWC was measured at 170/minute heart-rate using a bicycle ergometer and an electro-cardiogram. "Sedentary" youths were "shopkeepers and students with no sports or agricultural activity"; physically active" youths did at least "2-3 hours of daily moderate work" or were "agricultural laborers [or] full-time farmers". The report also concluded that "Nutritional status during early life had no influence on [AWC] except in so far as it had an influence on current body size" (p. 142).

39. For example, the 16 physically active youths with earlier moderate CHR (average height 150 cm., weight 36.7 kg., at age 15.5 years) averaged 23.4% higher AWC than the 7 sedentary youths with a normal CHR record (average height 159 cm., weight 29.5 kg., at age 15.3). Ibid., p. 141.

40. The following standards are in regular use (percentages of the observations on the 50th percentile at Harvard): Weight/age: Gomez or Harvard: 75-90% mild, 60-75% moderate, below 60% severe (Chen, 1981, p.60, and Mason et al., 1982, p.III-37-B), or 80-?% first-degree, 70-80% second-degree, below 60% third-degree (Ebrahim, 1979, p. 75). Wellcome: 60-80% "underweight" (or "kwashiorkor"); below 60% "marasmic, with no edema" (or "marasmic kwashiorkor") - respectively Mason et al. (Ebrahim). Height/age: Harvard: 90-95% mild, 85-90% moderate, below 80% severe (Chen). Gomez: 1st degree, 85-92.5%; 2nd, 75-85%; 3rd, below 75% (Seckler, p. 26). Weight/height: 80-90% mild, 70-80% moderate, below 70% severe (Sukhatme, 1981, p. 42, citing Chen).

41. National Institute of Nutrition (1975). Productivity (bundles per day) was significantly linked to weight (r=.7208), height (r= .4333) and lean weight (r=.7358); but the link to height became insignificant when either weight or lean weight was held constant (first-order partials).

42. Nutrition Reviews (1980), p. 145: "The reduced work performance was more likely due to their current and persistent undernutrition than a consequence of early childhood malnutrition".

43. Berg (1981) cites several studies relating smallness - not necessarily due to childhood undernutrition - to low work output. However, except for extreme conditions, the evidence given here suggests that this link can be removed by build-up of adult levels of diet, physical activity, and therefore lean mass and muscle efficiency.

44. Chen et al., cited in Sukhatme (1981), Table 8, and discussed there and in Nutrition Reviews (1981). Mason et al. (1982), p. III-38-B, discuss Chen and other sources, but appear to suggest - contrary to Chen's evidence and without citing counter-evidence - that "mild-to-moderate" anthropometric shortfalls also increase risk of mortality.

45. We assume they adopt spending patterns roughly typical of, for their area, families with their own income (or outlay) per CU.

46. Populations with gene-pools lowering average stature are probably mythical. They reach "Western" size norms with economic development (Miller, 1980, p. 27), which removes the survival-drawbacks of big and/or high-BMR persons within a given gene-pool by providing (a) lower infection rates, (b) less "fat-penalising" (p. 17) work - and (c) more food. But is (c) alone - beyond the point where it increases survival-rates, or mental or physical performance - desirable just because Big is Beautiful? My value-judgement is "No" - but we must avoid "double standards, one for us and one for them" (Miller, 1979, p. 200).

47. To be analysed in my 1983 World Bank Staff Working Paper, Demography and Poverty.

48. Prema et al. (1981), pp. 897-8; Frisch (1978), esp. pp. 2205, (1980), pp. 2395-9, and (1982), pp. 1272-3. See also Frisch et al. (1981), esp. pp. 1561-21, and Wyshak et al.(1982), pp. 1033-5. British research also confirms that, despite zero intake increases during pregnancy and small ones in lactation, requirements for both were fully met, proving "subtle changes in activity ... enhanced efficiency of metabolism, or ... substantial [improvements] in non-lactational ... physiological efficiency": Whitehead et al. (1981), p. 265.

49. "A supplement of 200 kcal/day ... reduced [incidence of] low birthweight by 75% and associated mortality by 50%"(Rohde, 1982a, p. 9, citing A. Lechtig et al., 1975).

50. Beaton and Ghasseimi (1982), p. 909. There is no reason to assume that pregnant women would be likelier to avoid these effects than pre-school children, and in view of the "clear trigger level [for birthweight gain] at 20,000 calories during pregnancy ... any substantial leakage can be expected to result in program failure" (Rohde, 1982a, p. 4).

51. This is because $((2) + (500) + (98)(820))/100$ is 105% of $((15)(500) + (85)(820))/100$.

52. This is the same sort of effect, for age-structure data, as reported on p. 14, sec. 2, para. 3 (use of national, or even upper-income, weight-for-age data to assess caloric requirements of the poor).

53. My WBSWP, Labour, the Poor and the Ultra-Poor (1983), discusses the evidence.

54. In Botswana in 1977-8, over 40% of apparently available working time was unused, due mainly to seasonal slack in agriculture (Lipton, 1978).

55. Most nutritionists regard intra-personal variation as a more important potential reducer of true undernutrition. Interpersonal variation in DER, even if correlated with intake variation, would not as a matter as statistical necesssity reduce numbers undernourished, but realistic worked examples strongly suggest it would in practice (fn.65), as does the argument of Beaton (Appendix to Reutlinger and Alderman, 1980).

56. This refers to the three successive energy requirements estimates (most recently FAO/WHO, 1973), not to the FAO's Fourth World Food Survey, FAO Statistics Series No.11, Rome, 1977. This seeks to adjust caloric requirements downward, principally to allow for interpersonal and intrapersonal DER variations. See, however, Miller (1979), p. 20, for list of surveys of "whole populations" of "apparently healthy individuals who customarily consume less than the FAO [Fourth World Food Survey] critical limit of 1.2 BMR".

57. Sukhatme (1982), pp. 2, 14, states that, in estimating proportions of persons undernourished, India's National Nutrition Monitoring Board has "not carried out ... adjustments ... for age, sex, body weight and level of activity", i.e. presumably had assumed that there was no interpersonal variability to reduce any of these in poor households below the Indian average; and that the same is true (less seriously?) within outlay-per-person-group averages for the National Sample Survey.

58. In other words, lowering the LDC average DER (to allow for an over-high base for average DC requirements, and for over-generous "translation" from DC to LDC averages) may reduce the proportion, or the period, that intake can acceptably fall below the new, lower, LDC average. I am indebted to Dr. Denis Casley, formerly of the FAO Fourth World Food Survey team and now at the World Bank, for this important note of caution.

59. Modification is needed to the extent that newer estimates already reduce average DER, claimed to be just acceptable for any particular ASAG, to allow for the fact that many people below the old (higher) levels were also below average DERs. Such reduction already took place in the FAO's Fourth World Food Survey, to reach their minimum of 1.2 BMR (instead of the former 1.5); despite Srinivasan (1981), p. 2, it may be acceptable for this survey to make no further allowance for variability.

60. 95% of Indian men weighing 55 kg, and engaged in moderate activity, will maintain body weight at rates varying between 1900 and 3200 kcal/day - a coefficient of variation of 13% (Sukhatme, 1981, p. 6). Note that the true weight average is 49.1 kg (fns. 27-28), giving a 1700-2850 range.

61. That is, the probability that a random observation is between any two intake-levels is unaffected by the requirements-levels of the person observed; and vice versa.

62. (a) Adult diets (or work) are much less likely to alter a given body-fat weight if it is due to many fat cells - which may often be genetic (Greenwood et al., 1981, p. 78) - than if it is due to enlarged fat cells (Sims, p.14; Björntop, p.58; Faust, esp. p.56; all 1981); could exceptionally few fat cells assist survival in LDCs? (b) Brown adipose tissue has been shown to be present and active in, and variable among, humans; "a defect in, or an absence of, BAT would predispose to obesity" (Rothwell and Stock, 1979, p. 34), in Western sedentary subjects at least - but to adaptive survival, in LDCs, among poor laborers and their children) otherwise at risk of undernourishment? (c) Work on diet-induced thermogenesis, too, seeks ways to help fat people (by stimulating it) - but why not hungry people (by retarding it)?

63. Regular intense effort, as in peak seasons for laborers in manually-based agriculture, raises BMR by up to 25% for 15 hours: Runner's World, 1980, p. 44. See also Miller (1982), p. 195.

64. In that severe undereating is a much surer killer, above some caloric deficiency per kg/day, than is an equally severe caloric overdose prolonged for a given period.

65. A crudely simplified symmetric example may help. Suppose 900 people are equally divided among three requirements states, R cals/kg/day, 1.1R, and 0.9R; and among three intake states, I cals/kg/day, 1.1I, and 0.9I. Let I = R. If the requirements state is independent of the intake state, the expected outcome is that 300 people have intake below requirements (200 by 10-11%, 100 by 22%). If "1.1R" persons have 1.05 times the average probability of being at 1.1I, and only .95 times the average probability of being at 0.9I - and conversely for "0.9R" people - then an expected 295 people have intake below requirements (200 by 10-11%, 95 by 22%).

66. A weight-maintaining response, possibly glandular, that normally adjusts appetite and thus intake to requirements. For the reverse homeostasis, adjusting conversion-efficiency and thus requirements to earlier intake, see pp. 31-34. On some models covariance between energy and requirements need not reduce - may indeed slightly increase - the incidence of undernutrition in a population (hence the apparently paradoxical result for India in Reutlinger and Alderman, 1980, p. 15); but Beaton's Appendix to this paper, p. 24, shows why such an effect is in practice unlikely, as does fn. 65 above.

67. Nutrition Reviews, 1980a, pp. 338-9, citing Edmundson; see also McCance, 1978, p. 403.

68. A comparison of brown-fat activity and fat/lean ratios - one or both presumably higher among the high-BMR group, unless all the difference was due to intrapersonal variation - would be fascinating.

69. See above, fn. 62. This effect is separate from short-period homeostatic adjustments (pp. 31-34 below).

70. It is not suggested that genetic mutations could acquire significance in the evolutionarily short time-scale of a dozen or so generations; but certainly poor families with "wrong" (BMR-irresponsive) genes could die out. Compare fn. 46.

71. Such families may well "run to fat" in later economic development; if they curtail caloric intakes as development reduces the effort-intensity of their output, their BMRs fall in (outmoded) evolutionary response!

72. For example, correction for body weight reduced the 2SD-level of variation in requirements only from 1750-3350 to 1900-3200 (about the 2550 mean) for Indian adult males, so that the coefficient of variation fell only from 16% to 13% (Sukhatme, 1981, p. 6).

73. In overfed humans, responsive decreases in food-to-work conversion efficiency - and hence reduction in the accumulation of body weight - "have been ascribed to increases in diet-induced thermogenesis" (Rothwell and Stock, 1979, p. 32). Here we ask if the reverse process may work when caloric intake falls.

74. "Training effect" may matter, since hunting, lumbering and many sorts of peak farmwork involve energy requirements and durations comparable to light athletic training: see da Guzman, 1976, p. 91, Table II. On training-diet relations in aerobic glycolysis, see Sharp, 1980, pp. 23-5.

75. See Sukhatme, 1978, 1982, and his main primary evidence: Acheson et al., 1980; Edholm et al., 1970; Edmundson, 1979, 1980; Pranajpe, 1979; and Tilve, 1979.

76. In particular, we do not know how long people of different ages can tolerate, without harm, shortfalls of various sizes.

77. Srinivasan (1980). Few people can tolerate many days of caloric intake 30% below ASAG average requirements without serious harm: Keys et al., 1950, pp. 727, 853.

78. "The threshold values encompassing the range [of homeostasis are] necessarily indefinite ... by 'threshold' I do not imply that there is any sharp discontinuity in the distribution. All that is meant is that the risk of undernutrition remains about the same over a wide, though limited, range of intakes" (Sukhatme, 1982, p. 29).

79. They also imply, correctly, that the same person can be in different categories at different seasons of a year.

80. The number clinically undernourished at any moment is far less than (a) the number ever undernourished, (b) the number at risk of under-nourishment. Nobody knows how much less.

81. See above, fn. 75 ; the Edholm study of military trainees, the Edmundson study of Javanese farmers, Acheson's study of researchers in Antartica, all exclude children. Taylor and Beaton (1980) hypothesize that undernourished children reduce play and inhibit psychomotor develop-ment, rather than adjusting BMR homeostatically. However, Kielmann et al., in Taylor et al., 1978, p. 3-27, conclude from the Narangwal data that "nutritional deficiency in the range commonly encountered in a rural, ambulatory community seemed not to be associated with permanent psychomotor impairment".

82. See Dandekar, 1982, p. 206, for criticism along these lines. It is, however, not correct to dismiss Sukhatme's switch from a 3SD to a 2SD borderline as arbitrary; see Sukhatme, 1982, pp. 5-7.

83. Sukhatme (1978, p. 1383) argued that variability and homeostasis reduced the proportions undernourished in urban Maharashtra from 63% to 33%, and for all-India to 20% (rural), 25% (urban). He concludes (1980, p. 1103) that at most "15 to 20 percent of India's population can be considered undernourished for want of adequate income".

84. The derivation from household data of individual adjustments, given various assumptions on household shortfall and intra-household dis-tribution, is a statistical issue. See Sukhatme, 1981, p. 1322; Dandekar, 1982, pp. 206-7.

85. The Pan-American Health Organisation (cf. Newland, 1981, p. 20) argued 10-15 years ago that undernutrition contributed to one in three deaths among under-fives in Latin America. Such deaths may be due largely to anorexia and underfeeding during dysentery. New knowledge would now suggest a sharply lower figure for deaths due to poverty-induced hunger, even in very poor LDCs. See fn. 123 on the role of oral rehydration and inoculation in preventing these deaths.

86. This is (a) because a more stringent borderline inevitably makes shortfalls more serious, (b) due to the impact of disturbance outside the limits of homeostasis (see fn. 77 above).

87.   Ruzicka, 1982, pp. 6-7 and Table 2; the agreed fall in fertility
      since 1961-70, plus the steady rate of population growth (and little net
      immigration), implies a similar fall in mortality. If evenly spread
      over age-groups, this would take the probability of survival from
      birth to age 20 to .854(M), .838(F), in the 1970s.

88.   Sukhatme (1980) who adds that the observed proportion is smaller;
      this is confirmed below (p. 59).

89.   This note refers to all NSS data used here.   (i) Due care is taken
      to avoid statements based on very small subsamples in cells. (ii) The
      NSS data are not very reliable on "sensitive" matters like tenure and
      credit. On consumption expenditure, several cross-checks are included
      in the survey design. (iii) As for typicality, 1972-3 and 1974-5 were
      well below trend for food output (itself almost flat), and 1971-2 and
      1973-4 well above trend, in all three States; thus cereal output in
      Rajasthan was 7.1 million t. (1970-1), 5.0m. (1971-2, 4.2m. (1972-3),
      5.4m. (1973-4) and 4.0m. (1974-5); in Gujarat the respective data
      were 4.2m., 4.1m., 2.1m., 3.4m., and 2.0m.; and Maharashtra 4.8m.,
      4.3m., 2.6m., 6.2m., and 4.0m. (Government of India, 1969 to 1977.)

90.   The 2400 figure (fn. 27) was for sedentary adult males. This 2700
      norm, used by NSS, is just over 60% towards the "moderately active"
      figure (fns. 27-8).

91.   Big differences in averages in calorie intakes, as between groups
      that each cover a large range of outlay per consumer, do not of course
      imply any discontinuity.

92.   See my World Bank Staff Working Paper, Demography and Poverty, 1983.

93.   Norms vary. Ahluwalia, Carter and Chenery, as explained in Chenery,
      1979, p. 459, cited 2150 cals/person/day as the Indian minimal
      requirement "most widely used". NSS data give a ratio of persons
      to consumer units of 0.796 (rural), 0.807 (urban)(M.R. Rao, 1979, p. 112)
      i.e. - assuming 80% of the population rural - 0.798 overall, implying
      a requirement of (2150 ÷ 0.798) or 2694 kcals/CU/day, or virtually
      2700.

94.   In Table 2 the calculation is made as follows: "9 out of every 100
      rural households spending 0-15 Rs/person/month are not calorie-
      deficient. Assuming they get exactly 2300 kcals/CU/day, and have the
      same number of CUs as the 91 remaining (and calorie-deficient) house-
      holds spending 0-15 Rs/month, that leaves [(1493) (100) - (2300)(9)]
      ÷ 91 or 1413 kcals/CU/day, for these (91% of 4.6%) or 4.2% of rural
      persons", and so on for each rural and urban outlay-group. Since
      (on NSS assumptions, which then excluded nonrandom variability in
      requirements) the 2300 kcal/day assumption, for the adequately fed
      in each outlay group, is a minimum, the number of cals/CU "left over"
      for the underfed is a maximum; hence the "at most" in the text.
      The "apparently" is to allow for the fact that some employees, on
      some days, receive food incorrectly counted into their employers'
      consumption in the NSS.

95.   Sarvekshana, Jan. 1979, pp. S305, S369. Requirements for pregnancy
      and lactation may also raise total kcal need, relative to intake,
      among the poorest, especially rurally, due to higher (a) child/adult
      ratios, (b) infant and child mortality rates, and (c) female/male
      ratios in child-bearing age-groups; see, however, pp. 11 and 21-23
      above.

96. Or even negative; extra purchased food may be outweighed by reduced breast-feeding (Reutlinger and Selowsky, 1976, pp. 24-38). Cf. Bhalla, 1980, p. 42; Seckler, 1980, on stunting; see, however, fn. 122 below for a more complex view of the evidence for intra-household food bias against children.

97. Visaria, 1978, pp. 15, 99-100. Proportions below the "poverty line" (about Rs. 40 of monthly per-person consumer expenditure, MPCE) reported among landless households, households owning 0.61-0.99 acres, owning 1.00-2.49 ac., and owning 2.50-4.99 ac. were, respectively, 37%, 44%, 40%, and 41% in Gujarat; and 60%, 64%, 67% and 59% in rural Maharashtra. (Above 5 ac./household, the incidence of poverty clearly fell sharply as owned-holding size rose).

98. See Table 3, note. These ten showed farm outlays above total outlays, leaving consumer outlays apparently negative; probably an exceptional outlay on a farm output, made in the survey week, was financed by an unrecorded loan. Apart from these ten, six showed exceptionally high weekly consumer outlay: in Doka, all 40 households spent below 27.0 shillings per CU; in Dan Mahawayi, all 34 spent below 31.5 sh/CU/week, except for one at 42.0 and one at 95.1; in Hanwa, all 36 spent below 27.4 sh/CU/week, but four "outsiders" spent 36.9, 41.1, 41.5 and 92.4. These outlays reflect exceptional, probably loan-financed, purchases in the survey week. These six households are included in Table 3, but not in later tables, or in discussion relating kcal intakes to "poverty" assessed by outlay.

99. Stewart, 1980, pp. 19-20. The primary sources cited are, respectively, data from the Institute of Child Health, Lagos, supplied to ILO; Tomkins et al., 1978; and a paper prepared for a joint Population Council/UNFPA workshop in October 1978.

100. The above elasticities for the quartile are, respectively, .67, .74 and .61.

101. A study of 150 farm households from one district in Gujarat showed that a rise in the proportion of persons aged under 11 (and in no older age-group) significantly altered (increased) the proportion of both outlay and income devoted to food : Deolalikar, 1981, pp. 15, 17, 23.

102. Rouis, 1980, p. 20; 1978 monthly cost of sufficient calories, per person, urban, N 13.70; all basic needs, N 22.80; rural, N 9.10; all basic needs, N 11.30. Ratio 60% urban, 80% rural. Rouis shows that, if it is reasonable to assume that the urban poor can devote 70% (instead of 60%) of outlay to food, urban persons below the poverty line - i.e. unable to afford an adequate diet - fall by 15%.

103. In Nigeria, too, the alleged urban poverty line turns out to be double the rural level! See above, fn. 102.

104. (a) Repayment of interest on loans should be deducted before such ratios are calculated; this is not always done. (b) Low ratios may be consistent with undernutrition if "food habits" reduce outlay on food, e.g. by reducing kcal intake to family members with dysentery; but this is not usefully defined as undernutrition due to income inadequate to meet basic kcal needs. For this purpose an 80% food/outlay ratio is still in order.

105. For the six households in Doka not undernourished, yet spending only 2.9-4 sh/CU/week, the ratio of food expenditure to total household expenditure was: no. 3, 67%; no. 26, 85%; no. 48, 82%; no. 58, 80%; no. 64, 87%; and no. 82, 93% (Simmons, 1976, pp. 97-100). They were also buying very cheap calories.

106. Comparison statewise with all-India data from Table 6 shows that some of the apparent variety, among all-India outlay-per-head groups, in food/nonfood outlay ratios is due to an "ecological fallacy" and does not correspond to variations in specific States. Also elasticity equations, especially statewise fit much better if the lowest outlay groups are excluded.

107. Bhanoji Rao, 1981. The uncertainty about the turning-point, and the very small differences in food/outlay ratios about that point, make this proposal rather risky until basic survey data improve.

108. Sarvekshana (June 1979) shows the following proportions of rural households (starting from the lowest outlay-per-person group) for which food/outlay ratio fails to fall as outlay-per-person rises: Assam, of 2591 sample households, 7.7%-15.5% (depending on whether we exclude or include, in the "non-Engelian" group, households in the turning-point outlay-group; these have a higher food/outlay ratio than the next poorer group, but a lower ratio than all better-off groups, to which Engel's Law does apply); Bihar (5739), 8.2-14.5%; Gujarat (3381), 16.6-31.9%; Haryana (2233), 14.3-28.5%; Himachal P. (1190), 3.3-13.2%; Jammu and Kashmir (4307), 0.7-2.2%; Kerala (3789), 20.6-31.1%; Madhya P. (5739), 7.6-14.4%; Maharashtra (5249), 10.8-17.2%; Manipur (782), 15.0-36.7%; Meghalaya (1025), 3.1-4.9%; Karnataka (3333), 25.2-41.1%; Orissa (3312), 6.2-15.5%; Punjab (3064) 6.3-13.6%; Rajasthan (2285), 10.4-15.9%; Tamil Nadu (5984), 3.1-7.0%; Tripura (1085), 14.8-31.8%; Uttar P. (7985), 7.3-13.7%; W. Bengal (4895), 28.7-40.3%. Urban percentages are consistently lower.

109. Only 2 weeks out of 52 could be measured for diets. These were always about 6 months apart and spaced over a year, but inevitably the relationship between the two weeks will have differed among households (sometimes one was a peak week, sometimes the other was a trough, etc.).

110. Such "undernourishment" is reduced by the factors considered on pp. 9-34.

111. Morley et al., 1968. These seasonal concerns remain, even if requirements for average pregnancies are being met (pp.11, 21-24). For evidence that the poorest are likeliest to rely heavily on income from working on others' land - with its non-shiftable peaks - see Lipton, 1983a.

112. The poorest region; in the others, Engel's Law applied to the whole data sets.

113. Considerably below the 75-85% ratios usually found at levels of poverty such as these; perhaps non-food prices were relatively higher.

114. Other surveys show that such outlay-per-household data do not rank households, or even deciles, well by poverty (outlay per person or CU), but that big groups of households, as in this survey, are correctly ranked.

115. Tabor, 1979, p. 17. Calorie consumption in the poorest three groups was, however, implausibly low (ibid., p. 16).

116. At this stage, all these (and starchy roots) are aggregated; substitution effects among basic staples would, I hypothesise (fn. 117),
strengthen the argument. Pulses include some high-value products,
and are thus not here aggregated with cereals as basic staples. On
p.46 we look at the information on "poverty and hunger" given by
Indian households' reliance on NSS Food Group I, which includes
cereals and cereal substitutes, sugar and jaggery, and (unfortunately,
because they are seldom cheap) potatoes.

117. On pp. 45-47 only, short-cut definitions are used: of "undernourishment" and "adequate nourishment", to mean kcaloric ingestion
respectively below and above 2300 kcals/CU/day; of "the ultra-poor",
to mean the lowest two outlay groups in Table 8; and of "the cheapest
foods" to mean the Indian NSS's Food Group 1 (see under Table 8).
Unlike Dr Shah I exclude Food Group 2 (pulses, nuts and seeds) when
assessing reliance on the cheapest kcal sources, because such foods
are often quite costly per kcal; the choice does not make much
difference to the argument.

118. See Schofield, 1979, p. 73; for fifty villages with data on income-
per-person and food/total outlay ratios, r is only -0.23 (significant
only at 10%). Of course, ingenuity with functional forms (e.g. in
Deolalikar, 1981) can obtain much better fits, but often lacks theoretical
justification; cannot (or ought not to) conceal the complete failure
of the Law for the ultra-poor; and leaves the deep puzzle of why, in
the same outlay group, some are undernourished while others escape
(cf. Shah, 1979).

119. Schofield, 1979, p. 91, citing a study by R. Singh in a Lucknow,
U.P., village, and one by W. Collins in Northern Nigeria.

120. Central Statistical Office, 1976, p. 12; Lipton, 1979, Vol. II,
pp. 164-5; and, for Nigeria, Rouis, 1980, p. 15. It is not clear
what role meat plays in the basic diet used by Rouis to construct
his 'poverty line', which is a cheaper diet than the one discussed
here (the only one analysed for composition by Rouis). In this diet,
beans are a much cheaper protein source than meat or fish.

121. Visaria, 1980, pp. 65, 68-9. The association of polygamy (in a society
where Islam prohibits most female earnings) with relative affluence
may explain why, in N. Nigeria, poorer families do not show higher
child/adult or female/male ratios.

122. Gopalan, 1968, shows 50% higher incidence of PEM among children of
fourth or higher than of third or lower birth order. Significant
similar effects are described in Kielmann et al., in Taylor et al,
pp. 3-25; Antrobus; Morley et al.; K.V. Rao; and Gopalan, 1971.

123. Nor can we infer that, at least in moderately poor households, more
food intake - especially if mediated by the uncertain, albeit very
desirable, means of higher family income - is a cost-effective way to
cure such deprivation. The "GOBI package" - growth charts, oral rehydration, breastfeeding, inoculation - may well be quicker, cheaper
and more effective, at least where dehydration is a major problem
in diarrhea. See UNICEF, 1983.

124. Schofield, 1979, p. 83. Data on proportionate fulfilment of requirements tend in the opposite direction (p. 87), but are much less
convincing due to the very shaky nature of estimates of requirements
- even now, but much more when these surveys were undertaken. The
differences were significant at 5% in the African surveys and 1% in
the Latin American surveys, but (on more up-to-date requirements
estimates) no significant sex differences in intake/requirements
ratios were found among rural Guatemalan 3-year-olds (Martorell,
Klein and Delgado, 1980, p. 223).

125. Chen, Haq and D'Souza, 1981, pp. 57, 60, 62. It is wrong to read this
paper as showing "that females were fed less, relative to their size,
than males at all stages of life [, especially] the very young and
the elderly" (Newland, 1981, pp. 29-30; my italics).

126. National Institute of Nutrition, 1977, p. 165. The National Nutrition
Monitoring Bureau's Report for 1980 (1981, p. 49) lists requirements -
these appear to have been set above true average requirements,
especially for women (and children), compared to FAO/WHO, 1973, streng-
thening the evidence against selective female underfeeding. See
above, fn. 28.

127. Pinstrup-Anderson, 1981, p. 12. Ryan's Indian (ICRISAT) evidence
suggests that better anthropometric status (partly nutritional in
origin) enables men, but not women, to earn significantly higher wages;
see Lipton, 1983a.

128. These differences may be associated with different levels of medical
care, or nutrition, or both.

129. This argument, being probabilistic, is affected by neither (a) the
margin of doubt surrounding much of the recent evidence discussed
in this paper, nor (b) the fact that damage does not suddenly set in
at (i) the same cals/kg. for all in any ASAG or (ii) an arbitrary
anthropo-arithmetic boundary between severe and MMU.

130. In such surveys, it is not always the same children who are weighed
in the various seasonal or monthly rounds. If, say, 3% of children
in a given village and round suffer severe undernutrition, the
danger is greater if most children are in the same condition at all
rounds - but the "target" requiring priority intervention is smaller.

131. Or of a degree of caloric shortfall which (even allowing for possible
adaptive increases in food-work conversion efficiency - pp. 31-33
would if prolonged induce severe undernutrition.

132. In particular, the economic analysis usually accepted - as assumptions
- the conclusions from earlier experiments on earlier high-yielding
varieties. This grossly exaggerated, for upcoming varieties, the
risk (in face of pest attack and moisture stress); the requirement
for tightly-defined environmental and managerial conditioning; and
the benefits from fixed-proportions input packages. Many errors
followed, notably that of "blaming" the technology (not the socio-
political environments) for maldistributions following its introduction (Lipton, 1978A 1979).

133. See above, p. 8.   Even today, at least one of the world's leading experts remains unconvinced. Meanwhile, certainly, Indian crop research stations in the 1960s and 1970s diverted massive resources to breeding varieties for high protein content, when local research had revealed hardly any <u>human</u> diets with adequate calories but inadequate proteins.

134. Although this was in fact the basis for the scaling-down in FAO, 1977.

135. When they overcome theoretical objections to interpersonal comparison of utility; but otherwise little policy advice is possible. "Extra outlay is worth the same whoever gets it" is simply one (odd) inter-personal weighting.

136. Of the large outlays on India's SFDA-MFAL programmes for small farmers (2.5-5 acres), marginal farmers (0.1-2.5 acres) and the landless, 6 per cent appears to have reached households most of whose income was derived from hired labor (Bailur, 1983): the poorest households, for the most part.

137. Diversion. from foods to non-foods by a target household, presumably chosen in the light of its members' perception of needs, is - apart from the issue of intra-family distribution of benefit - not a major problem. Diversion from the needy to others is.

138. Damage in this respect could, of course, be compensated by benefits, including benefits that peaked in the hungry season, elsewhere in the economy.

139. Conversely, large central stores - while occasionally justified - are perhaps unduly favored by financing agencies; they frequently transfer grain, with substantial losses and costs, from places of food need to places of political pressure.

BIBLIOGRAPHY

K. Acheson et al., 'A longitudinal study of body weight and body fat in Antarctica', American Journal of Clinical Nutrition (hereafter AJCN), 33, 1980.

M. Ahluwalia, N. Carter and A. Chenery, 'Growth and poverty in developing countries', Journal of Development Economics, September 1979.

R. Andres, 'Aging, diabetes and obesity; studies of normality', Mount Sinai Journal of Medicine, 48, 6, November-December 1981.

A. Antrobus, 'Child growth and related factors in a rural community', Journal of Tropical Paediatrics, 17, 1971.

G. Bailur, Ministry of Rural Development, Government of India, personal communication, February 1983.

A. Bang, 'Minimum wages for agricultural labor', Economic and Political Weekly (hereafter EPW), XVI, 33, August 18, 1979.

M. Bapat and N. Crook, '"Housing and slums in Poona" reconsidered: the possible alternatives', EPW, XIV, 33, August 18, 1979.

S. Batliwala, 'Rural energy scarcity and nutrition: a new perspective', EPW, XVII, 9 , February 27, 1981.

G. Beaton and H. Ghasseimi, 'Preschool feeding programs', AJCN, 35, 4 (Suppl.) April 1982.

J. Bengoa and G. Denosa, 'Prevalence of protein-calorie malnutrition, 1963 to 1973', Protein Advisory Group Bulletin, 4, 1, 1974.

E. Betancourt, Las Carencias Nutricionales en Colombia, Revision 1977, ICBF, 1977, cited in Mohan et al.

A. Berg, The Nutrition Factor, Brookings, 1973.

————, Malnourished People; A Policy View, World Bank, June 1981.

J. Bergsman, Income Distribution and Poverty in Mexico, World Bank Staff Working Paper (hereafter WBSWP) No. 395, June 1980.

S. Bhalla, Measurement of Poverty: Issues and Methods, mimeo, World Bank, 1980.

P. Björntop, 'Adipocyte precursor cells', in Björntop et al., 1981.

P. Björntop et al. (eds.), Recent Advances in Obesity Research: III, Libbey (London), 1981.

K. Blaxter (ed.), Food Chains in Human Nutrition, Applied Science Publishers, 1980.

F. Bleiberg et al., 'Energy output of female farmers in Upper Volta', British Journal of Nutrition (hereafter BJN), 43, 1, 1980.

Botswana, Government of, Central Statistical Office, Rural Income Distribution Survey 1975, Gaborone, 1976.

Botswana, Government of, Central Statistical Office, Poverty Datum Line for Urban Areas of Botswana, 1976.

R. Boxall et al., Prevention of Farm-level Foodgrain Storage Losses in India, IDS Research Report, Brighton, 1978.

J. Brosek (ed.), Behavioral Effects of Energy and Protein Deficits, (Proceedings of the International Nutrition Conference, November-December 1977), DHEW-National Institute of Health, Bethsada, NIH Publication No. 79-1906, 1979.

D. Buss, 'Some consequences of the new UK "recommended daily amounts of food energy and nutrients" for evaluating food consumption surveys', Journal of Human Nutrition, 33, 5, 1979.

W. Bussink et al., Poverty and the Development of Human Resources: Regional Perspectives, WBSWP No. 406, July 1980.

M. Buvinic et al., (eds.), Women's Issues in Third World Poverty, Johns Hopkins, 1982.

P. Cantrelle and H. Lendon, 'Breastfeeding, mortality in children, and fertility in a rural zone of Senegal', Population Studies, 25, 2, 1971.

A. Carloni, 'Sex disparities in the distribution of food within rural households', Food and Nutrition, I, 1, 1981.

R. Cassen, India: Population, Economy, Society, MacMillan, 1978.

S. Chakrabarti and M. Panda, 'Measurement of incidence of undernutrition', EPW, XVI, 31, August 1, 1981.

R. Chambers, letter to D. Gwatkin, May 7, 1981.

R. Chambers, R. Longhurst and A. Pacey, Seasonal Dimensions to Rural Poverty, Pinter, 1981.

R. Chandra, 'Malnutrition and infection', paper at UNU/MIT Conference on nutrition and development, mimeo, MIT/UNU, Cambridge (Mass.), 1980 (to be published in book edited by M. Wallerstein, 1983).

——————, 'Immunodeficiency in undernutrition and overnutrition', Nutrition Reviews, 39, 6, 1981.

P. Chaudhuri, 'Nutrition and health problems and policies: women and children in India', mimeo, British Society for Population Studies, Oxford Conference, December 1982.

L. Chen, E. Haq and S. D'Souza, 'Sex bias in the family allocation of food and health care in rural Bangladesh', Population and Development Review, 7, 1, 1981.

L. Chen et al., 'Anthropometric assessment of PEM and subsequent risk of mortality ...', AJCN, 33, cited in Sukhatme (1981).

H. Chenery, Structural Change and Development Policy, Oxford, 1979.

R. Chitre and V. Agte, 'Concept of essential amino-acids in human nutrition', Pt. I, Indian Journal of Nutrition and Dietetics (hereafter IJND), 15, June 6, 1978.

R. Chitre and M. Dikshit, 'Concept ...', Pt. III, _ibid._, 15, August 8, 1978.

A. Chowdhury, S. Huffman and L. Chen, 'Agriculture and Nutrition in Matlab Thana, Bangladesh', in Chambers, Longhurst and Pacey.

Consolazio, cited in Petrasek.

N. Crook and T. Dyson, 'Data on seasonality of births and deaths', in Chambers, Longhurst and Pacey.

K. Dandekar and M. Sathe, 'Employment Guarantee Scheme and food-for-work program', EPW, XV, 15, April 12, 1980.

V. Dandekar, 'On measurement of poverty', EPW, XVI, 30, July 25, 1981.

——————, 'On measurement of undernutrition', EPW, XVII, 6, February 6, 1980.

V. Dandekar and N. Rath, _Poverty in India_, Poona, 1971.

S. Davidson _et al._, _Human Nutrition and Dietetics_ (6th ed.), Churchill Livingstone, 1975.

D. Davies, 'Human Development in Sub-Saharan Africa', in Bussink _et al._

A. Deaton, 'Inequality and needs: some experimental results for Sri Lanka', mimeo, Living Standards Measurement Survey, World Bank, 1980.

A. Deolalikar, 'Impact of family size and composition on household demand for consumption goods, saving, and leisure', presented at Population Association of America, March 1981, mimeo, Yale University.

R. Devadas _et al._, 'Nutritional profile of selected adolescent and adult women athletes', 16, December 12, 1979.

A. Downs, _Who are the Urban Poor?_, Committee for Economic Development, Supplementary Paper No. 26, New York, 1970.

E. Downs, 'Nutritional dwarfing: a syndrome of early protein-calorie malnutrition', AJCN, 15, March 1964.

B. Drasor _et al._, 'Diarrheal diseases', in Chambers, Longhurst and Pacey.

J. Durnin and R. Passmore, _Energy, Work and Leisure_, Heinemann, 1967.

G. Ebrahim, 'The problems of undernutrition', in R.J. Jarrett (ed.), _Nutrition and Disease_, Croom Helm, 1979.

D. Edholm et al., 'Food intake and energy expenditure of army recruits', BJN, 24, 1970.

W. Edmundson, 'Adaptation to Undernutrition', _Social Science and Medicine_, 140, 1980.

——————, 'Individual variation and BMR in East Java', _Ecology of Food and Nutrition_, 8, 1979.

P. Engle, C. Yarborough, J. Townsend and R. Klein, 'Sex differences in the effect of nutrition and social environment on mental development in rural Guatemala', mimeo, California Polytechnic State University, San Luis Obispo, 1981.

FAO, Energy and Protein Requirements: Report of a Joint FAO/WHO Expert Committee, FAO, Rome, 1973 (hereafter FAO/WHO).

——, Handbook on Human Nutritional Requirements, Rome, 1974.

——, Fourth World Food Survey, Food and Nutrition Series No. 10, Rome, 1977.

I. Faust, 'Factors which affect adipocyte formation in the rat', in Björntop et al.

A. Ferro-Luzzi et al., 'Food intake, its relationship to body weight and age, and its apparent nutritional adequacy in New Guinean children', ACJN, 28, December 1975.

J. Field, 'The importance of context: nutrition planning and development recommendations', in McLaren (ed.).

R. Fox, A study of Energy Expenditure of Africans in Rural Activities, Ph.D (Unpub.), University of London, 1953.

H. Freeman et al., 'Nutrition and cognitive development among rural Guatemalan children', American Journal of Public Health, 70, 12, December 1980.

R. Frisch, 'Population, food intake and fertility', Science, 199, January 6, 1978.

——————, 'Pubertal adipose tissue: is it necessary for normal sexual maturation?', Federation Proceedings, 39, 7, May 15, 1980.

——————, 'Malnutrition and fertility', Science, 215, March 5, 1982.

R. Frisch et al., 'Delayed menarche and amenorrhea of college athletes in relation to age at onset of training', Journal of the American Medical Association, 246, 14, October 2, 1981.

C. Geissler and D. Miller, 'Nutrition and GNP: a comparison of problems in Thailand and the Philippines', Food Policy, August 1982.

M. Gersovitz et al., 'Validity of the 24-hour dietary recall and 7-day record for group comparisons', Journal of the American Dietetic Association, 73, 1, 1978.

C. Goodloe and S. Tabor, 'The household expenditure survey of Bangladesh', USDA, mimeo, 1979.

C. Gopalan, 'Health proboems in pre-school children: III', Indian Journal of Tropical Paediatrics, 14, 1968.

——————, Lancet, 1969, 1.

——————, 'Family size and nutrition', National Institute of Nutrition, Hyderabad, 1971.

——————, reported in The Guardian, December 29, 1982.

G. Graham et al., 'Determinants of growth among poor children: nutrient intake-achieved growth relationships', AJCN, 34, April, 1981.

J. Grant, The State of the World's Children, UNICEF, December 1982.

R. Grawe, 'Human Resources in Asia', in Poverty and Development of Human Resources: Regional Perspectives, WBSWP No. 408.

M. Greeley, 'Rural technology, rural institutions and the rural poorest: the case of rice processing in Bangladesh', in Greeley and Howes.

M. Greeley and M. Howes (eds.) Rural Technology, Rural Institutions and the Rural Poorest, CIRDAP/IDS, Dacca, 1982.

M. Greenwood et al., 'Adipose tissue and genetic obesity', in Björntop et al.

L. Gulati, 'Rationing in a peri-urban community: case-study of a squatter habitat (Trivandrum), EPW, XII, 12, March 19, 1977.

Gujarat, Government of, Central Research Bureau, Village Development Surveys: Fifteen Adivasi Villages of Gujarat, 1975 (data for 1970-71).

M. da Guzman, 'Recent development in energy requirements of Filipinos', Philippine Journal of Nutrition, XXIX, 3, July-September 1976.

L. Harbert and P. Scandizzo, Food Distribution and Nutritional Intervention: the case of Chile, WBSWP No. 512, May 1982.

J. Harrington, 'Nutritional stress and economic responsibility: a study of Nigerian women', in M. Buvinic et al. (eds.).

N. Hicks, 'Sector priorities in meeting basic needs: some statistical evidence', World Development, 10, 6, 1982.

E. Hipsley, 'Metabolic studies in New Guineans', Technical Papers No. 162, South Pacific Commission, Noumea (New Caledonia), 1969.

J. Howell (ed.), Borrowers and Lenders, ODI (London), 1980.

M. Howes, 'The creation and appropriation of value in irrigated agriculture: a comparison of the deep tubewell and the handpump in rural Bangladesh', in Greeley and Howes (EDS) 1982.

ICMR (Indian Council for Medical Research), Studies on Pre-school Children, Technical Report Series No. 26, New Delhi, 1977.

ILO/JASPA, First Things First: Basic Needs in Nigeria, Addis Ababa, 1980.

India, Government of, Central Statistical Office, National Sample Survey, 26th Round 1971-72, Vol. 1 (No. 238).

——————————————, Ministry of Agriculture, Estimates of Area and Production of Principal Crops in India, 58th to 65th editions, Directorate of Economics and Statistics, Delhi, 1969 to 1977.

——————————————, Sixth Five Year Plan 1980-1985, Planning Commission, New Delhi, 1981.

Indian National Nutrition Monitoring Bureau, Report for the Year 1980, National Institute of Nutrition, ICMR, Hyderabad, 1981.

P. Isenman, 'Basic needs: the case of Sri Lanka', World Development, 10, 6, 1982.

A. Keys et al., The Biology of Human Starvation, University of Minneapolis, 1950.

R. Korte, 'Protein versus energy in Papua New Guinea', No. 6, Nutrition Reports, Department of Public Health, Post Moresby, 1974.

——————, 'The nutritional and health status of the Mwea-Tekere Irrigation Settlement', in H. Kraut and H.-D. Cremer (eds.).

A. Kielmann and Curcio, cited in A. Kielmann et al., Malnutrition, Infection, Growth and Development: The Narangwal Experience, World Bank, 1981.

A. Kielmann and L. McCord, 'Weight-for-age as an index of risk of death in children', The Lancet, June 10, 1978.

A. Kielmann et al., 'The Narangwal experiment in interactions of nutrition and infections: II. Morbidity and mortality effects', Indian Journal of Medical Research, 68 (Suppl.), December 1978.

R. Klein, Relationship of Pre-School Nutritional Status, Family Socio-economic Status and Pre-School Intellectual Ability to School Performance and School Age Intellectual Ability, mimeo, INCAP, 1981.

J. Kreysler and C. Schlage, 'The Nutrition situation in the Pangani Basin', in H. Kraut and H.-D. Cremer (eds.).

O. Knudsen and P. Scandizzo, 'The demand for calories in developing countries', American Journal of Agricultural Economics, 64, 1, February 1982.

H. Kraut and H.-D. Cremer (eds.) Investigations into Health and Nutrition in East Africa, Weltforum-Verlag, Munich, 1969.

I. Kravis et al., World Product and Income: International Comparisons of Real Gross Product, World Bank/Johns Hopkins, 1982.

S. Kumar, 'Role of the household economy in determining child nutrition at low income levels: a case study of Kerala', Occasional Paper No. 95, Division of Nutritional Sciences, Cornell, November 1977.

——————, 'Nutrition concerns for food policy in Africa', mimeo, IFPRI, Ibadan, 1981.

A. Lechtig et al., 'Influence of food supplementation during pregnancy', Proceedings of 9th International Congress on Nutrition, Mexico, 1973, 2, Basle (Karger), 1975.

D. Lee, Climate and Economic Development in the Tropics, Harper, 1957.

M. Lipton, Why Poor People Stay Poor, Temple Smith, 1977.

——————, 'Interfarm, interregional and farm-nonfarm income distribution: the impact of the new cereal varieties', World Development, 6, 3, 1978a.

——————, Botswana: Employment and Labor Use, Ministry of Finance, Gaborone, 1979.

M. Lipton, 'The technology, the system and the poor: the case of the new cereal varieties', in Development of Societies: the next 25 years, ISS, Martinus Nijhoff, The Hague, 1979a.

——————, 'Rural credit, farm finance and village households', in J. Howell (ed.).

——————, Demography and Poverty, WBSWP, World Bank, 1983.

——————, Labor, the poor and the ultra-poor, WBSWP, World Bank, 1983a.

R. Longhurst, Work, Nutrition and Child Malnutrition in a North Nigerian Village, D.Phil (unpub.), Sussex University, 1981.

R. Longhurst and P. Payne, 'Seasonal aspects of nutrition', in Chambers, Longhurst and Pacey.

S. Margen and R. Ogar (eds.), Progress in Human Nutrition, Vol. 2, AVI (Westport), 1978.

R. Martorell, R. Klein and H. Delgado, 'Improved nutrition and its effects on anthropometric indicators of nutritional status', Nutritional Reports International, 21, 2, 1980.

Mason et al., Nutrition Surveillance, Cornell University Agriculture Experiment Station (Department of Nutritional Sciences), 1982.

R. McCance, 'How much do we really know about requirements for energy and protein?', IJND, 15, 12, December 1978.

I. McGregor, 'The health of young children in a West African (Gambian) Village', Transactions of the Royal Society of Tropical Medicine and Hygiene, 62, 3, 1962.

D. McLaren, 'The great protein fiasco', The Lancet, 1974, 2.

D. McLaren (ed.), Nutrition in the Community (2nd ed.), Wiley, 1981.

J. Mencher, 'The lessons and non-lessons of Kerala', EPW, Special Number October 1980.

D. Miller, 'Prevalence of nutritional problems in the world', Proceedings of Nutritional Society, 1979, 38.

——————, 'Factors affecting energy expenditure', Proceedings of Nutritional Society, 1982, 41.

——————, 'Man's demand for energy', in Blaxter (ed.).

A. Mitra, India's Population: Aspects of Quality and Control, ICSSR/Family Planning Foundation, Vol. 1, 1978.

——————, 'Revolution by redefinition of parameters', in Margen and Ogar.

R. Mohan et al., Measuring Urban Malnutrition and Poverty in Colombia, WBSWP No. 447, World Bank, 1981.

D. Morley et al., 'Factors influencing growth and nutritional status of infants and young children in a Nigerian village', Transactions of the Royal Society of Tropical Medicine and Hygiene, 62, 2, 1968.

M. Morris, Measuring the Condition of the World's Poor: the PQLI Index, Pergamon, 1979.

D. Naismith et al., 'Carbohydrate conservation in the obese: a theory to explain the ease of weight gain', Annals of Nutrition and Metabolism, 25, 1, 1982.

National Institute of Nutrition (India), Annual Report 1975, Indian Council of Medical Research, Hyderabad, 1976.

————————————————————, Annual Report 1976, Hyderabad, 1977.

————————————————————, Annual Report 1978, Hyderabad, 1979.

National Nutrition Monitoring Bureau (India), Report for the year 1978, Hyderabad, 1979.

————————————————————, Report for the year 1980, Hyderabad, 1981.

K. Newland, Infant Mortality and the Health of Societies, Worldwatch Paper No. 147, Washington DC, December 1981.

J. Neel, 'Diabetes mellitus: a "thrifty" genotype rendered detrimental by "progress"?', American Journal of Human Genetics, 14, 1962.

D. Nicholls, 'Brown adipose tissue mitochondria', Biochemica et Biophysica Acta, 549, 1979.

B. Nichols, 'Reply to letter by Hirschhorn', AJCN, 31, November 1978.

Nutrition Reviews, Editorial, 38, 4, April 1980.

————————————, ibid., 38, 10, October (1980a).

————————————, ibid., 39, 11, November 1981.

S. Onchere and R. Sloof, 'Nutrition and Disease in Machakos District, Kenya', in Chambers, Longhurst and Pacey.

R. Palmour, 'Multifactorial components in cultural-biological interactions', in Margen and Ogar.

W. Paddock, Famine 1975!, Little Brown, Boston, 1967.

R. Patel, Afawa Village, Sardar Patel University (Agro-economic Research Centre for Gujarat and Rajasthan), Anand, 1962.

P. Payne and A. Dugdale, 'Patterns of lean and fat deposition in adults', Nature, 266, 1977, No. 5600.

R. Petrasek, 'Influence of climatic conditions on energy and nutrient requirements', Progress in Food and Nutrition Science, 2, 11/12, 1978.

P. Pinstrup-Anderson, Nutritional Consequences of Agricultural Projects, WBSWP No. 456, World Bank, 1981.

T. Poleman, 'Quantifying the nutrition situation in developing countries', Food Research Institute Studies, XVIII, 1, 1981.

S. Pranajpe, Time Series Analysis of Daily Dietary Intake and Nutrient Output, Ph.D. (unpub.), Poona University, 1980.

K. Prema et al., 'Changes in anthropological indices of nutritional status in lactating women', Nutrition Reports International, 24, November 5, 1981.

S. Preston (ed.), Biological and Social Aspects of Mortality and the Length of Life, Ordina (Liege), 1982.

M. Rao, 'Nutrition situation in India during 1971-72', Sarvekshana, January 1979.

V. Bhanoji Rao, 'Measurement of deprivation and poverty based on the proportion spent on food', World Development, 9, 4, 1981.

J. Rawls, A Theory of Justice, Harvard, 1971.

V. Reddy et al., AJCN, 29, January 1976.

S. Reutlinger and M. Selowsky, Malnutrition and Poverty: Magnitude and Policy Options, World Bank Occasional Paper No. 23, Johns Hopkins, 1976.

J. Rohde, Why the Other Half Dies, Leonard Parsons Memorial Lecture, mimeo, University of Birmingham, March 15, 1982.

——————, 'Community-based nutrition programs', mimeo, UNICEF, New York, September (1982a).

M. Rosenzweig and T. Schultz, 'Market opportunity, genetic endowments and the intrafamily distribution of resources: child survival in rural India', Center Discussion Paper No. 347, Economic Growth Center, Yale University, 1980.

N. Rothwell and M. Stock, 'A role for brown adipose tissue in diet-induced thermogenesis', Nature, 281, September 6 1979.

M. Rouis, Nigeria: Income Distribution and Poverty Profiles, mimeo, World Bank, June 5 1980.

Runner's World, September 1980.

L. Ruzicka, 'Mortality in India', mimeo, British Society for Population Studies, Oxford Conference, December 1982.

S. Schofield, 'Seasonal factors affecting nutrition in different age groups, and especially pre-school children', Journal of Development Studies, 11, 1, 1974.

——————, Development and the Problems of Village Nutrition, Croom Helm, 1979.

D. Seckler, 'Small but healthy', mimeo, Ford Foundation, New Delhi, 1980; reprinted in Sukhatme (ed.).

M. Selowsky, 'Nutrition, health and education: the economic significance of complementarities at early ages', mimeo, International Economic Association Conference, Mexico, 1980.

A.K. Sen, Levels of Poverty: Policy and Change, WBSWP No. 401, World Bank, 1980.

————, Poverty and Famine, Oxford, 1981.

N. Scrimshaw et al., 'Protein requirements of man: variations in obligatory urinary and faecal nitrogen losses in young men', Journal of Nutrition, 102, 1972.

C. Shah, 'Food preferences and nutrition: a perspective on poverty'; Presidential Address, Indian Society of Agricultural Economics, Bangalore, 1979.

C. Sharp, 'How to feed your hungry muscles', Running, July 1980.

E. Simmons, Calorie and Protein Intakes in Three Villages of Zaria Province, May 1970-July 1971, Samaru Miscellaneous Paper No. 55, Ahmadu Bello University, 1976.

————, Rural Household Expenditures in Three Villages of Zaria Province, Samaru Miscellaneous Paper No. 56, Ahmadu Bello University, 1976.

E. Sims, 'Hypertension and obesity: mechanisms and management', in Björntop et al. (eds.).

G. Solimano and M. Vine, 'Malnutrition, infection and infant mortality', in Preston (ed.).

C. Soman, 'Interrelationship between fertility, mortality and nutrition - the Kerala experience', in Sukhatme (ed.).

T. Srinivasan, Malnutrition: Some Measurement and Policy Issues, WBSWP No. 373, World Bank, 1980.

T. Srinivasan and P. Bardhan, Poverty and Income Distribution in India, Statistical Publishing Society, Calcutta, 1974.

F. Stewart, Basic Needs in Nigeria, mimeo, west Africa Division, World Bank, 1980.

P. Sukhatme, 'Malnutrition and Poverty', Ninth L.B. Shastri Memorial Lecture, Indian Agricultural Research Institute, New Delhi, 1977.

————, 'Assessment of adequacy of diets at different income levels', EPW, XII, 31-3, August 1978.

————, 'Nutrition policy: need for reorientation', EPW, XV, 26, June 28, 1980.

————, Relationship Between Malnutrition and Poverty, Indian Association of Social Science Institutions, First National Conference on Social Sciences, Delhi, January 12-15, 1981.

————, 'Measurement of undernutrition', mimeo, Maharashtra Association for Cultivation of Science, Pune, 1982.

P. Sukhatme (ed.), New Concepts in Nutrition and their Implications for Policy, Maharashtra Assocation for the Cultivation of Science, Pune, 1982.

S. Tabor, 'Susenas-V; preliminary evaluation of consumption trends and nutritional status', USDA, mimeo, 1979.

—————, 'Notes on the Brazilian consumption and expenditure survey', USDA, mimeo, 1980 (?).

J. Tanner, Foetus into Man, Open Books, London, 1978.

C. Taylor et al., 'The Narangwal experiment on interactions of nutrition and infections: 1. Project design and effects upon growth', Indian Journal of Medical Research, 68 (Suppl.), December 1978.

L. Taylor and G. Beaton, Report of a Workshop on the Uses of Energy and Protein Requirement Estimates in Economic Planning, UN University/MIT, Cambridge (Mass.), mimeo, 1980.

S. Tilve, 'Comparison of questionnaire and weighment methods in diet surveys', IJND, 15, 1, January 1978.

—————, Studies in Variation in Intake and Balance, Ph.D (unpub.), Poona University, 1979.

A. Tomkins, 'Folate malnutrition in tropical areas', Transactions of the Royal Society of Tropical Medicine and Hygiene, 73, 1979.

A. Tomkins et al., 'Water supply and nutritional status in rural Northern Nigeria', Transactions of the Royal Society of Tropical Medicine and Hygiene, 72, 3, 1978.

B. Torún et al. (eds.), UNU World Hunger Programme, Food and Nutrition Bulletin: supplements, No 5: Protein-energy requirements of developing countries: evaluation of new data, 1981.

UN, Demographic Yearbook 1979, New York, 1980.

UNICEF, Report on the State of the World's Children, New York, January 1981.

W. van Steenbergen et al., 'Lactation performance of Akamba mothers, Kenya', Journal of Tropical Paediatrics and Environmental Child Health, 1980.

V. Vidyanagar and V. Vyas, Ankodia Village, Resurveys of Indian Villages, Sardar Patel University, Anand, No. 1, 1969.

P. Visaria, Size of landholding, living standards and employment in rural Western India, 1972-73, Working Paper No. 3, Joint ESCAP-IBRD project on the evaluation of Asian data on income distribution, Washington, October 1978.

—————, Poverty and living standards in Asia, Living Standards Measurement Survey, Working Paper No. 2, World Bank, 1980.

R. Whitehead et al., 'Recommended dietary amounts of energy for pregnancy and lactation in the UK', in   Torún et al. (eds.).

E. Widdowson, 'Long-term individual dietary surveys', British Journal of Nutrition, 9, 1947.

G. Wood, The Socialisation of Minor Irrigation in Bangladesh, Proshika, Dacca, 1982.

World Bank, <u>World Development Report</u>, 1980.

——————————, <u>World Tables</u> (2nd ed.), Johns Hopkins (for World Bank), Baltimore, 1980.

G. Wyshak <u>et al</u>., 'Evidence for a secular trend in the age of menarche', <u>New England Journal of Medicine</u>, <u>306</u>, 17, 1982.

T. Yeshwanth and R. Rajagopalan, 'Consumption of cereals and shifts from inferior to superior cereals: a case study', <u>Khadigramdyog</u>, June 1964.

World Bank Publications of Related Interest

Analyzing the Impact of Health Services: Project Experiences from India, Ghana, and Thailand
Rashid Faruqee

Reviews four categories of health indicators (environment, services offered, services received, and changes in mortality, morbidity, and nutritional status) in order to evaluate the impact of health projects in India, Ghana, and Thailand.

World Bank Staff Working Paper No. 546. 1982. 44 pages.

ISBN 0-8213-0117-9. $3.00.

Benefits and Costs of Food Distribution Policies: The India Case
Pasquale L. Scandizzo and Gurushri Swamy

Analyzes some of the characteristics and the main consequences of the food distribution policies followed by the Indian government and provides a quantification and a cost-benefit analysis of their effects on consumers, producers, and the government budget.

World Bank Staff Working Paper No. 509. August 1982. 54 pages.

ISBN 0-8213-0011-3. $3.00.

Confronting Urban Malnutrition: The Design of Nutrition Programs
James E. Austin

Describes a framework for systematically carrying out urban nutrition programs that examines several key considerations in nutrition education, on-site feeding, take-home feeding, nutrient-dense foods, ration shops, food coupons, fortification, direct nutrient dosage, and food processing and distribution.

The Johns Hopkins University Press, 1980. 136 pages.

LC 79-3705. ISBN 0-8018-2261-0, $6.50 (£4.50) paperback.

The Costs and Benefits of Family Planning Programs
George C. Zaidan

A technique for measuring the economic returns from investing in population control, with an appraisal of inherent assumptions and limitations.

The Johns Hopkins University Press, 1971. 62 pages (including bibliography).

LC 70-155166. ISBN 0-8018-1317-4, $4.00 (£2.40) paperback.

Demographic Aspects of Migration in West Africa —Volume 1
K. C. Zachariah and others

Background data on migration in four English-speaking countries: Ghana, Sierra Leone, Liberia, and The Gambia. A regional analysis based on these studies is presented in *Migration in West Africa: Demographic Aspects.*

World Bank Staff Working Paper No. 414. September 1980. vi + 363 pages (including statistical annexes, bibliography).

Stock No. WP-0414. $15.00.

Demographic Aspects of Migration in West Africa —Volume 2
K. C. Zachariah and others

Background data on migration in four French-speaking countries: Ivory Coast, Upper Volta, Senegal, and Togo. A regional analysis based on

these studies is presented in *Migration in West Africa: Demographic Aspects.*

World Bank Staff Working Paper No. 415. September 1980. vi + 385 pages (including statistical annexes, bibliography).

Stock No. WP-0415. $15.00.

Economic Motivation versus City Lights: Testing Hypotheses about Inter-Changwat Migration in Thailand
Fred Arnold and Susan H. Cochrane

World Bank Staff Working Paper No. 416. September 1980. 41 pages (including footnotes, references).

Stock No. WP-0416. $3.00.

Economics of Supplemental Feeding of Malnourished Children: Leakages, Costs, and Benefits
Odin K. Knudsen

Analyzes some of the economic issues involved in the supplemental feeding of malnourished children. Demonstrates that supplemental feeding programs are economically justified if minimum improvements in mortality rates and more substantial increases in productivity take place.

World Bank Staff Working Paper No. 451. April 1981. iv + 76 pages.

Stock No. WP-0451. $3.00.

Experiments in Family Planning: Lessons from the Developing World
Roberto Cuca and Catherine S. Pierce

A comprehensive review of experimental efforts in the developing world to determine more effective ways of providing family planning services.

The Johns Hopkins University Press, 1978. 276 pages (including bibliography, index of experiments).

LC 77-16596. ISBN 0-8018-2013-8, $19.50 (£11.50) hardcover; ISBN 0-8018-2014-6, $8.95 (£4.00) paperback.

Family Planning Programs: An Evaluation of Experience
Roberto Cuca

World Bank Staff Working Paper No. 345. July 1979. xii + 134 pages (including 2 annexes, references).

Stock No. WP-0345. $5.00.

Fertility and Education: What Do We Really Know?
Susan H. Cochrane

A model identifying the many channels through which education might act to determine fertility and a review of the evidence of the relation between education and the intervening variables in the model that affect fertility.

The Johns Hopkins University Press, 1979. 188 pages (including bibliography, index).

LC 78-26070. ISBN 0-8018-2140-1, $6.95 (£4.75) paperback.

Fertility and Its Regulation in Bangladesh
R. Amin and
Rashid Faruqee

World Bank Staff Working Paper No. 383. April 1980. iv + 50 pages (including references).

Stock No. WP-0383. $3.00.

NEW

Food Distribution and Nutrition Intervention: The Case of Chile
Lloyd Harbert and
Pasquale L. Scandizzo

The impact of Chile's Complementary Feeding Program (CFP), both on the direct and indirect beneficiaries, is analyzed. Describes Chile's major nutrition intervention programs and establishes the relative importance of the CFP in terms of budgetary expenditures and number of beneficiaries reached. Reviews briefly the programs past limitations, recent reforms, and potential effectiveness.

World Bank Staff Working Paper No. 512. May 1982. v + 45 pages (including bibliography, annex).

ISBN 0-8213-0001-6. $3.00.

Health
Fredrick Golladay,
coordinating author

Draws on experience gained from health components of seventy World Bank projects in forty-four countries between 1975 and 1978. Emphasizes the disproportionately high expenditures incurred on curative medicine, maintenance of expensive hospitals, and sophisticated training of medical personnel at the cost of preventive care for the majority of the people. Points out that low-cost health care systems are feasible and recommends that the Bank begin regular and direct lending for health, in addition to having health components as part of projects in other sectors.

Sector Policy Paper. February 1980. 90 pages (including 8 annexes, 4 figures, map). English, French, Japanese, Spanish, and Arabic.

Stock Nos. PP-8001-E, PP-8001-F, PP-8001-J, PP-8001-S, PP-8001-A. $5.00.

Health Issues and Policies in the Developing Countries
Fredrick Golladay

World Bank Staff Working Paper No. 412. August 1980. ii + 53 pages.

Stock No. WP-0412. $3.00.

NEW

Health, Nutrition, and Family Planning in India: A Survey of Experiments and Special Projects
Rashid Faruqee and
Ethna Johnson

Surveys fourteen experiments and special projects in health, nutrition, and family planning in India and proposes guidelines for future Bank projects on the basis of the survey.

World Bank Staff Working Paper No. 507. February 1982. xi + 97 pages (including references).

Stock No. WP-0507. $5.00.

NEW

Integrating Family Planning with Health Services: Does It Help?
Rashid Faruqee

Analyzes the findings of an experiment carried out in Narangwal, a village in Punjab, India, between 1968 and 1974 related to health care and family planning. The World Bank collaborated with The Johns Hopkins University in analyzing this data from one of the best known and well-documented field experiments in health care and family planning in the world.

World Bank Staff Working Paper No. 515. September 1982. 47 pages. ISBN 0-8213-0003-2. $3.00.

Kenya: Population and Development

(See description under *Country Studies* listing.)

Malnourished People: A Policy View

(See description under *Development* listing.)

Malnutrition and Poverty: Magnitude and Policy Options
Shlomo Reutlinger and
Marcelo Selowsky

The first large research effort in the World Bank to determine the global dimension of malnutrition.

The Johns Hopkins University Press, 1976; 2nd printing, 1978. 94 pages (including 5 appendixes).

LC 76-17240. ISBN 0-8018-1868-0, $4.75 (£2.85) paperback.

Spanish: Desnutrición y pobreza: magnitudes y opciones de política. Editorial Tecnos, 1977.

ISBN 84-309-0726-2, 380 pesetas.

Measuring Urban Malnutrition and Poverty: A Case Study of Bogota and Cali, Colombia
Rakesh Mohan,
M. Wilhelm Wagner,
and Jorge Garcia

Attempts to measure the extent of malnutrition and poverty in the cities of Bogota and Cali, Colombia. One of five papers resulting from a research program entitled "City Study," a study of the workings of five major urban sectors in Colombia.

World Bank Staff Working Paper No. 447. April 1981. 80 pages (including bibliography, appendixes).

Stock No. WP-0447. $3.00.

Migration in West Africa: Demographic Aspects
K. C. Zachariah and Julien Condé

The first study of the large-scale movement of people in nine West African countries. Discusses the volume and direction of internal and external flows and the economic and social characteristics of migrants.

A joint World Bank-OECD study. Oxford University Press, 1981. 166 pages (including 22 maps, bibliography, index).

LC 80-21352. ISBN 0-19-520186-8, $19.95 (£10.50) hardcover; ISBN 0-19-520187-6, $8.95 (£4.50) paperback.

Nutrition and Food Needs in Developing Countries
Odin K. Knudsen and Pasquale L. Scandizzo

World Bank Staff Working Paper No. 328. May 1979. 73 pages (including 4 appendixes).

Stock No. WP-0328. $3.00.

Population and Poverty in the Developing World
Nancy Birdsall

World Bank Staff Working Paper No. 404. July 1980. 96 pages (including 2 appendixes, bibliography).

Stock No. WP-0404. $3.00.

Population Policies and Economic Development
Timothy King and others

The English-language edition is out of print.

Spanish: Políticas de población y desarrollo económico. Editorial Tecnos, 1975.

ISBN 84-309-0605-3, 440 pesetas.

Population Policy and Family Planning Programs: Trends in Policy and Administration
Kandiah Kanagaratnam and Catherine S. Pierce

World Bank Staff Working Paper No. 411. August 1980. iii + 22 pages (including footnotes).

Stock No. WP-0411. $3.00.

Regional Aspects of Family Planning and Fertility Behavior in Indonesia
Dov Chernichovsky and Oey Astra Meesook

Discusses the recent decline in Indonesia's population growth rate despite that country's relatively low level of income and socioeconomic development. Reviews the history and organization of the family planning program and attempts to identify those factors that have been responsible for its success and assesses its prospects for the future.

World Bank Staff Working Paper No. 462. May 1981. 62 pages (including appendix, references).

Stock No. WP-0462. $3.00.

REPRINTS

Health Care in the Developing World: Problems of Scarcity and Choice (Shattuck Lecture)
John R. Evans, Karen Lashman Hall, and Jeremy J. Warford

World Bank Reprint Series: Number 209. Reprinted from New England Journal of Medicine, vol. 305 (November 1981):1117-27.

Stock No. RP-0209. Free of charge.

Measurement of Deprivation and Poverty Based on the Proportion Spent on Food: An Exploratory Exercise
V.V. Bhanoji Rao

World Bank Reprint Series: Number 193. Reprinted from World Development, vol. 9, no. 4 (1981):337-53.

Stock No. RP-0193. Free of charge.

Nutrition, Health, and Education: The Economic Significance of Complementarities at Early Age
Marcelo Selowsky

World Bank Reprint Series: Number 218. Reprinted from Journal of Development Economics, vol. 9 (1981):331-46.

Stock No. RP-0218. Free of charge.

WORLD BANK PUBLICATIONS
ORDER FORM

SEND TO:
WORLD BANK PUBLICATIONS
P.O. BOX 37525
WASHINGTON, D.C. 20013
U.S.A.

or

WORLD BANK PUBLICATIONS
66, AVENUE D'IÉNA
75116 PARIS, FRANCE

Name: _____

Address: _____

_____

Stock or ISBN #	Author, Title	Qty.	Price	Total

Sub-Total Cost: _____

Postage & handling fee for more than two free items ($1.00 each): _____

Total copies: _____ Air mail surcharge ($2.00 each): _____

TOTAL PAYMENT ENCLOSED: _____

Make checks payable: WORLD BANK PUBLICATIONS

Prepayment on orders from individuals is requested. Purchase orders are accepted from booksellers, library suppliers, libraries, and institutions. All prices include cost of postage by the least expensive means. The prices and publication dates quoted in this Catalog are subject to change without notice.

No refunds will be given for items that cannot be filled. Credit will be applied towards future orders.

No more than two free publications will be provided without charge. Requests for additional copies will be filled at a charge of US $1.00 per copy to cover handling and postage costs.

Airmail delivery will require a prepayment of US $2.00 per copy.

Mail-order payment to the World Bank need not be in U.S. dollars, but the amount remitted must be at the rate of exchange on the day the order is placed. The World Bank will also accept Unesco coupons.